DO YOU 'REALLY' WANT TO GET BETTER?

DO YOU 'REALLY' WANT TO GET BETTER?

Learn To Eliminate Those Behaviors, Thoughts, & Feelings That Are Barriers To Your Happiness

Michael John Frank, Ph.D.

BridgeRock Press, 197 Strathearn Rd., Toronto, Ontario, Canada, M6C 1S3

Printed and Bound by University of Toronto Press, Inc.

Do You 'Really' Want To Get Better? is available from:

University of Toronto Press, Inc.
5201 Dufferin Street,
North York, Ontario, Canada.
M3H 5T8
Tel.: (416) 667-7791
Fax: (416) 667-7832

OR

University of Toronto Press, Inc.
340 Nagel Drive,
Cheektowaga, New York 14225 - 4731
Tel. & Fax: (716) 683-4547

Toll Free in Canada & U.S.: 1-800-565-9523

(8:30 a.m. - 5:00 p.m. e.t.)

Do You 'Really' Want To Get Better?

Printed & Bound in Canada

Canadian Cataloguing in Publication Data

Frank, Michael John, 1943-

Do You 'Really' Want To Get Better?: Learn To Eliminate Those Behaviors, Thoughts, & Feelings That Are Barriers To Your Happiness.

ISBN 0-9698769-0-4

1. Self-actualization (Psychology). 2. Self perception. I. Title.

BF637.S4F73 1995 158'.1 C94-932626-7

DEDICATION AND ACKNOWLEDGMENTS

With love, gratitude and appreciation I dedicate this book to a few very "special" persons who have provided much support and positive reinforcement in my life - my loving parents, Gertrude and Samuel Frank, my devoted brother Jeffrey, my loving Aunt Grace, and my cherished and beloved Christina.

When one writes a book, there are so many persons to thank who have been influential to the process and final product.

A scholarly debt of appreciation is owed to a former teacher, Professor Kenneth MacCorquodale, and to a long-time close friend and colleague, Dr. Grant Coulson.

Appreciation is extended to the many clients who helped shape the effectiveness of the content presented in this book. Their feedback on conceptual materials and their rapid improvement were most encouraging.

Special appreciation is extended to a dear friend, Judy Brock, for her feedback, encouragement and support.

Appreciation and thanks is extended to Nancy McKnight-Little, who read the manuscript carefully and offered encouragement and detailed suggestions for improvement, many of which were incorporated.

Thanks to Edyth Karwecki for her excellent typing.

"This is an eminently readable book that describes an approach that has proven effective in solving problems and should prove very useful to its readers. Therefore, highly recommended!"

- **Nathan H. Azrin, Ph.D.,** a distinguished Psychologist and foremost authority in the applied use of behavioral psychology.

"Dr. Frank's book is a clearly written and easily read amalgam of several techniques which are individually effective. The final product, however, has "Dr. Michael John Frank" written on it in bold. What Dr. Frank does, and what he describes, is a set of explicit procedures for helping the person change his/her life directly. The emphasis on "data, data, data" is refreshing in a field where "empathic listening" and "sympathy" will lead to years of return visits and no improvement. A great teacher once said to me that we should be practicing "science with heart". This book is an example. You should read this book because, if you don't, there are important things you won't know. Highly recommended."

- **Dr. Grant Coulson,** Chief Psychologist and Director of The Precision Learning Center, Toronto.

Learn How to ...

- **Rapidly eliminate depression and stop wasting time with therapies that don't work and drag on for years.**
- **Connect with good feelings and positive thoughts.**
- **Empower yourself and enhance self-esteem through effective behaviors.**
- **Separate your "self" from your mistakes.**
- **Rid yourself of fairy tale assumptions that are ruining your life.**
- **Rethink your problems by turning them upside down.**

TABLE OF CONTENTS

PREFACE

You are not alone. Regardless of how inadequate you feel, and regardless of how paralyzed your actions may be, realize that this is not uncommon. An optimism of change exists for you! This book takes the mystery out of many frustrating and painful problems by redefining them in terms of causes and effects. Some of these problems include depression, low self-esteem, anxiety, anger, and unhappiness. There is a focus on what causes them, how they are sustained, and how to eliminate them. It is the consequences of our actions, and not inner forces, that control behavior, moods and thoughts. Learn how to demystify your problem, and learn how to take immediate action to quickly "get better".

This book delivers! I will teach you two effective intervention strategies, and how to take measurements to monitor your progress. Behavioral Interventions target ineffective behaviors and losses of positive reinforcement. Disputational Interventions target what we say to ourselves about those losses. The "accepted" accuracy of these thoughts, and the personal meaning attached to them are how we upset ourselves. This meaning is determined by past consequences and by underlying assumptions about what we think "ought to be" and "must be". I will teach you to challenge the validity and legitimacy of your fairy tale assumptions that are obstructing happiness.

I will teach you to challenge and dispute thoughts of inadequacy and worthlessness, and to separate your mistakes from your "self". Focusing on performance and not the "self" makes 'blame' a non-issue. Failing is only a behavior and you are only human. Learn to focus on improving your performance without judging your "self". Don't demand perfection from an imperfect being.

No drug can change your underlying assumptions, beliefs and self-critical thoughts. No drug can teach you effective behaviors and skills. And, no drug can make your environment more positively reinforcing. If you **really** want to get better, only behavioral changes and active disputations can produce improvements that last.

An understanding and application of the concepts and strategies presented in this book have proved very effective in helping clients rapidly "get better", eliminate depression, and enhance self-esteem. They can do the same for you. Seize the moment. Let me help you to help yourself. Some of the clients who showed remarkable improvement after only a few sessions, had previously been on medication or had gone through years of traditional psychotherapies without much progress. Extraordinary? Not really. Why shouldn't effective treatments produce rapid improvement that lasts?

This raises two myths about psychotherapy.

- The first myth is that only long-term treatment produces effective results. In other words, effectiveness cannot be achieved within a brief period of time.

- The second myth is that short-term treatment is inevitably superficial. In other words, only long-term treatment can produce lasting benefits.

Effectiveness and lasting benefits of treatment have nothing to do with the duration of therapy. Such beliefs are myths. They are not facts and are not supported by evidence. If anything, long-term treatment merely demonstrates ineffective treatment. I know, from my own clinical practice, that when a treatment is effective, improvement occurs immediately and continues to gain momentum. I know this by setting measurable goals and taking frequent and repeated measurements of progress. Such measurements guide therapy toward effectiveness within a brief time period. If a treatment is not working, recorded data will indicate this and allow for timely revisions. Any therapy that does not systematically collect data and set measurable goals, is working in the dark and is basically bankrupt from the start.

Reading this book can guide you in becoming an effective agent of change toward "getting better" and eliminating unhappiness. I wish you well on that journey.

CHAPTER 1

LISA'S SEARCH FOR A THERAPIST

"I have been feeling depressed for many months now. I thought I could handle it myself, but I can't shake it. I need help but don't know where to turn. I don't even know exactly why I'm depressed. Maybe it's biological? Maybe it's just me. I don't do anything right. I'm just useless.

Damn it. Why won't it go away? My life is empty and meaningless and I'm miserable. It's unfair and not the way it should be.

Where to seek help? I know a few people who are being treated for depression. One has been going to a psychiatrist for thirteen years and the other one is on medication. They both appear as sick as ever. Are these my choices? I don't trust drugs and I don't want to make a career out of my depression. I just want to get better. Surely, there must be someone out there who can help me.

I made some enquiries. Tom, a co-worker, told me he's been seeing a psychiatrist for three and a half years that he highly recommends. "He's a great guy, caring and compassionate. It's so comforting to have someone listen," Tom repeated many times throughout our conversation.

When I asked why he still needed therapy after so many years, Tom replied, "It's a long process. That's just the way therapy works." Sensing my uneasiness with his answer, Tom added, "He says I'm still in denial and haven't yet resolved certain underlying psychodynamic conflicts." It sounded like horsefeathers to me, and I backed off.

The next day, while in tears, and sitting alone in the lunchroom, I heard my name called. Looking up, Mrs. Robertson was standing over me. She is a bubbly, bright executive in our office. I was so embarrassed.

She sat down, expressed concerns about my welfare, and asked if I wanted to talk about it. Into the conversation, Mrs. Robertson told me that she once suffered with depression. I was totally surprised. She seemed to be such a "together person".

I enquired how she overcame it. That's when Mrs. Robertson told me about Dr. Samuel. She explained that prior to seeing him she had wasted a lot of time and money with two other therapists who did nothing for her over a three year period."

"Actually I was getting worse," Mrs. Robertson said. "At that point, someone I respect very much recommended Dr. Samuel. Of course I was skeptical. I had lost hope in myself, my therapist and in any chance of ever getting better.

Perhaps out of desperation, I called and made an appointment. Starting with the first session, I started improving immediately! I know how incredible that sounds, but it's true. I had to fill out different tests. I remember my score on a Depression Inventory was 43. That's severe depression. At the beginning of the second session my score dropped to 27. And by the fourth session it was 8.

My mental health had returned, and I felt great. I continued to see Dr. Samuel for maybe two more sessions until certain goals of mine had been reached. At that point I felt confident enough to maintain the progress we had made together. That was four years ago.

Dr. Samuel taught me so much. But don't be fooled. I'm not always happy, but I've learned how not to be unhappy. He taught me how to create my own happiness and how to be an effective person. Setbacks and rejections no longer have the same impact they used to have."

"How is Dr. Samuel's approach so much different than the others?", asked Lisa. "Tell me more."

Mrs. Robertson replied. "First of all, it works, and it works quickly. Not just with me, but also with other clients I know about. Clients I've referred to him.

His therapy is very unconventional compared to others I've been exposed to. He cuts right through the high grass, explains the nature of the problem and presents solutions. Dr. Samuel is more like a **teacher-scientist-coach**. He taught me how to conceptualize and understand my problems and how to do something about them. He taught me to be effective.

We set goals for things I wanted and kept measurements of my progress. That was very helpful. He also showed me how to challenge and prove the falseness of beliefs I had about myself that were hurting me. We also challenged assumptions I had about the way I "should behave" and about my "expectations" of life.

Although I said his approach is unconventional, it should be the conventional treatment and not an exception. Another thing, Lisa, his sessions are not the customary fifty minute sessions. Each lasts for two hours."

"Mrs. Robertson, I noticed that you used the word "client" and not "patient". How come?"

"Interesting you picked up on that. Dr. Samuel always preferred the term **"client"** to **"patient"**. He explained that treating someone as a "patient" demands an unquestioning acceptance and dependence. "Trust me, I know best." On the other hand, treating someone as a "client" removes such dependency. It involves clients in the process of decision-making based on data. It gives them more power.

I remember Dr. Samuel once remarking on the current state of psychotherapy. He found it interesting that consumers of other professional services demand **accountability** in terms of results, the time it takes to achieve those results, and the cost involved. Yet in therapy this is usually ignored.

Dr. Samuel practices what he preaches. Repeated and frequent measurements of progress provide accountability."

"I like what I'm hearing," Lisa said. "Can you give me his number?"

Mrs. Robertson searched her purse and gave Lisa Dr. Samuel's card.

"Thanks for your concern, Mrs. Robertson."

"My pleasure Lisa. I know what depression is like. Let me know how things work out." Mrs. Robertson returned to her office.

"That afternoon I telephoned Dr. Samuel to make some enquiries and perhaps set up an appointment. To my surprise, he invited me to attend a small gathering in his office that Thursday evening. He said that he'll informally present his approach and answer any questions. I was delighted and could hardly wait.

I arrived at the office just before seven. Dr. Samuel greeted me at the door with a warm smile and handshake.

I entered. There were eight others already seated. The room had a comfortable yet scholarly appearance with wall to wall books.

I helped myself to a cup of coffee and cookies from a table in the corner, and sat down."

After a few moments, Dr. Samuel spoke. "Thank you for coming this evening. I'm going to give you useful information about depression, effective therapy, and answer any personal or general questions. Feel comfortable to interrupt me at any time.

Okay, let's begin."

CHAPTER **2**

MOTIVATION TO GET BETTER

"How many of you want a million dollars?" All hands went up. "How many of you are willing to work for it?" Only half raised their hands.

"Interesting", said Dr. Samuel. "We lost half. You may be thinking about the costs involved if you devoted your life to making money. There are also some benefits of your present life that you would have to give up.

How many of you want to get better? Again, all hands went up. Wanting money and wanting to get better do not necessarily imply a willingness to work toward these goals.

Sometimes I ask clients to separately rate "desire" and "commitment" on a ten-point scale. **Desire for change** is always rated 10 out of 10. On the other hand, a **commitment to work for change** is most often rated somewhere between a 4 to 8 out of 10. These clients lack a strong motivation to work for what they want. While it would be nice if it happened, getting well isn't a high priority in their lives.

The benefits of remaining depressed and the costs of what they would have to give up to get well, outweigh the costs of remaining depressed and the benefits of getting well. In other words, **there are often strong reinforcers for remaining depressed, and weaker reinforcers for getting well**. The struggle between these reinforcers will determine a client's **motivation** and commitment. That's all motivation is. There's no mystery to it. It's not a force that comes from within. **Motivation is an issue of reinforcement.**

Let's further examine and clarify the concept of motivation. The word "motivation" lacks precision and is somewhat vague and useless. For example, if we were told by Johnny's teacher that Johnny failed "because he wasn't motivated", what information have we really gained? It is more informative to be told that Johnny failed because he wasn't interested in the subject matter. More precisely, the subject matter did not hold reinforcing value for Johnny, and accordingly, he was unwilling to expend much effort.

A lack of motivation may also implicate inadequate rewards offered to Johnny for working hard. While grades may not be an appropriate incentive for Johnny, social reinforcers from the teacher and others, or some other incentive may be effective in getting Johnny to study, work hard and pass. There are also other plausibilities that can be explored.

The point is that the term "motivation" lumps all causal factors together and accordingly tells us nothing about Johnny's problem or how to correct it.

The term "motivation" describes a relationship between performance and the reinforcing value of some thing. Receiving a reinforcer of reinforcing value is dependent upon an adequate performance. To measure "motivation" we are actually measuring the effects of reinforcers on work or performance. If some thing has reinforcing value, then we will work to get it.

What are Johnny's reinforcers? This is a more constructive question to ask, instead of asking why he failed and referring to a lack of motivation as the cause. The term "motivation" adds nothing to an analysis of the problem. It merely clouds the issue and distracts us from searching for the real cause and controlling variables. It is a form of psycho-babble.

To repeat, motivation is an issue of reinforcement. It describes the <u>relationship</u> between a reinforcer and the behavior required to get that reinforcer.

Now that we have a better understanding of what motivation is, we can return to our discussion of motivation within therapy.

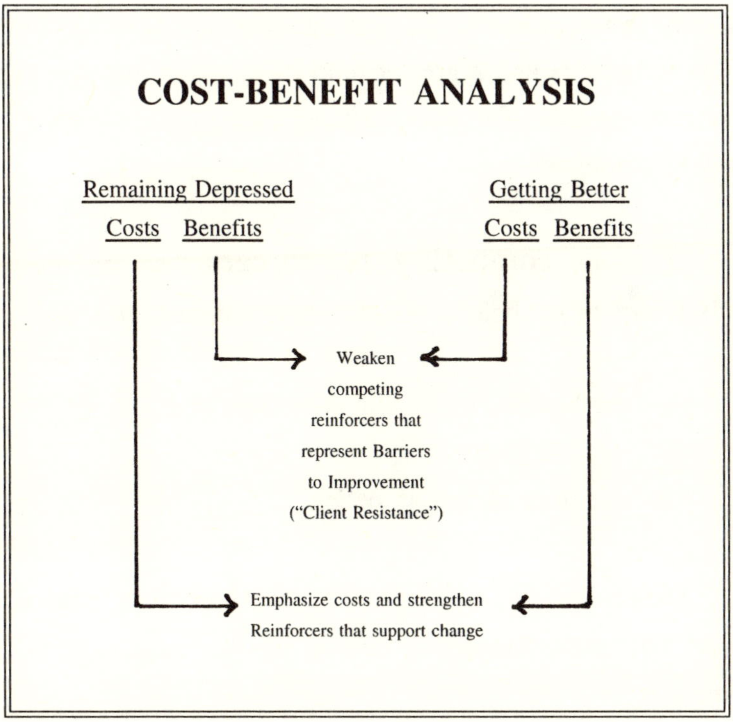

A therapist can enhance a client's motivation to work for change by emphasizing the costs of remaining depressed, strengthening the benefits of getting better, while simultaneously challenging and weakening the benefits of remaining depressed and the costs of getting better.

For therapy to be effective, a client's motivation must be dealt with early in the process. The key question is: Does getting well have more benefits and a greater reinforcing value than the benefits and reinforcing value for remaining depressed? The question is not as silly as it sounds.

There are **competing reinforcers** that can obstruct a client's efforts to get better. As already mentioned, they are:

(a) the benefits of staying depressed, and

(b) the costs of getting better.

These competing reinforcers represent **barriers** to therapeutic progress. It is the therapist's task to tip the balance in favor of "wellness".

Client Motivation Is The Therapist's Task

A group member asks a question. **"If someone isn't motivated to get better, then why seek therapy?"**

Dr. Samuel responds. "There are several reasons. First, as mentioned, there is a desire to get better and a hope that it can be a quick and easy fix. That is the allure of a "magic pill" such as Prozac. It's as if the client were saying to the therapist, "Let the magic begin. Do your thing but don't involve me."

Unfortunately, such a treatment is something that is done to clients. It is not a treatment that teaches clients what they can do for themselves. They remain dependent persons who are now dependent upon a physician and upon a drug about which they have little understanding. All they have to do is swallow. A dependency on others and a lack of control over influences in their lives is now further compounded by more dependencies and less control.

This contradicts a desired therapeutic goal of "independence" and is perhaps the first violation of a client's innocence and trust in such therapies.

A second reason clients enter therapy has less to do with getting better and more to do with the individualized comfort and nurturing they'll receive. These factors contribute very little to client improvement. Nevertheless, they must be very satisfying to some clients as is indicated by repeated visits to the same clinician over years and even decades.

It is a most interesting phenomenon. The psychiatric establishment has hoodwinked us to expect little and demand nothing. We have been taught to accept ineffective treatments and not hold the therapist accountable for wasted time and costs. This may be due to a client's innocence, trust and a lack of enlightenment to more effective approaches.

A third reason clients enter therapy is to gain "insight" into the mysteries of <u>why</u> they behave as they do. "Insight" does not lead to change. It is an ineffective form of treatment that can last for decades. For example, relating an early childhood molestation to a present-day avoidance of men does nothing to alter this behavior.

It is not unusual for clinicians to blame slow therapeutic progress on an unmotivated client. The preferred jargon is **"client resistance"**. Clients readily accept this blame, thereby adding another self-blame to their existing repertoire of hang-ups. More times than not, it's merely a therapist's poor excuse for ineffective treatment. No attempts are made to identify and remove those "resistances" that interfere with efforts toward improvement. Repeating again, client motivation is the therapist's task.

Competing reinforcers that inhibit progress often remain unquestioned and unchallenged. One of the therapist's first tasks is to identify these implicit barriers and express them explicitly to the client. This can be accomplished in a structured interview that uses a **cost-benefit analysis** as its framework.

Sympathy and attention are sometimes obvious competing reinforcers that sustain depression. Others are less obvious and more difficult to detect. Let's examine **some case studies that illustrate competing reinforcers that are less obvious.**

Molly came to me with moderate to severe depression. Her Depression Inventory Score was 31. She had previously been to a few psychiatrists over many years without much improvement. During our first session I was able to discern that Molly saw herself as a "supreme caretaker" in a world that didn't provide her with a choice.

This was her perceived role in life that was legitimized by society. Statements like "I must" and "I have no choice" were accepted as part of her inevitable reality. She devoted all her time and energies to the fulfillment of role obligations that she hated. After all, Molly's place in life was to please others. When Molly did things for herself that she enjoyed, she considered them as selfish acts and felt guilty.

Within the framework of a cost-benefit analysis, I asked Molly what she would lose or have to give up if she were no longer depressed. Molly paused for a few seconds and replied, "If I were no longer depressed, I wouldn't be able to read the newspaper any more. I really enjoy that. I would probably also have to give up my daily walks."

While these answers seem to make little sense on the surface, I immediately knew that we had just discovered a barrier to getting better. Reading the newspaper and long walks were "acceptable" while in a state of depression, but "unacceptable" otherwise. Expectations and demands from family members disappeared. Molly was no longer made to feel that she "must" meet previous role obligations. While Molly did not enjoy the depression, she did enjoy the liberation that came with it. In other words, there were reinforcers that were sustaining her present depression and were competing with positive reinforcers for getting well.

Molly's lack of progress in previous therapies may be partially explained by failure to identify and remove these existing barriers. In the first two sessions with Molly I focused on a treatment intervention that removed these competing reinforcers.

I knew I was on the right track by the data we collected. Molly's Depression Score improved from a 31, moderate to severe depression, to a 12, borderline depression, in two sessions. This verified the effectiveness of my treatment intervention. In the third session Molly's Depression Score improved again to a 6. A score of 10 or less is healthy-normal.

I can't emphasize enough the importance of monitoring progress, keeping data, and sharing this information with clients. Molly felt good about her accomplishments and I was able to check on the effectiveness of my intervention. If Molly had not shown improvement, I would have quickly made timely revisions.

Always allow the data to guide you. Throughout therapy I use many tests and many behavioral measures to guide treatment.

Psychiatrists and most clinicians do not keep data. This may partially explain their continuous ineffectiveness over years and decades with the same client, sometimes guaranteeing life-time careers for each. Unfortunately, only one gets paid. For what, I haven't yet figured out. It is the biggest con game in town that has been legitimized by the medical establishment and accepted by a deceived public.

But why should the public know any better? They see themselves as "patients" under the care of "experts" who tell them, "Trust me, progress is only years away." If clients act intelligently and question the lack of progress, they can always be befuddled with psycho-babble such as, "You won't get better until you overcome your denial and resolve those hidden psychodynamic conflicts."

Unfortunately psychiatrists get paid for whom they have been legitimated by society to be, and not for what they do. It is an attempt by the establishment to dignify ineffectiveness. Perhaps this is similar to the old witch doctors.

"Blind faith" over many years is a little much. You may say to me, "Yes, I agree, but what choice do I have? The psychiatrist is the 'expert' and knows about these things." The answer is that you don't have to know psychiatry to rate effective performance. Look at the data. What do the data say? Demand accountability and demand that measurements and data are kept. Data. Data. Data. Without data we can never correct mistakes or know when to quit. **PUT YOUR TRUST IN DATA.**

Consider a second case study that illustrates the conflict between the motivating forces to get well and competing reinforcers to remain depressed.

Louise was unemployed and without a career direction. She had perceived her life as meaningless and without purpose in a society that frowns upon
both. Others criticized and blamed her for not being productive and Louise blamed and criticized herself. In her eyes she was "worthless".

With the onset of depression there was an interesting shift of blame and responsibility for her unproductiveness. The depression and not Louise was the new focus of blame. This provided an acceptable excuse that temporarily let Louise off the hook. If the depression were to disappear overnight, she would again be held responsible for a lifestyle that was not condoned by many.

While we have not addressed the cause or treatment of her depression, we have identified existing reinforcers that will impede efforts to get better.

The competing reinforcers were eliminated and treatment began by having Louise challenge and dispute her thoughts of worthlessness, failure and purposelessness. Louise was confusing her societal worth with her self-worth. This is an important topic that we will discuss later. She was using society's criteria as comparative benchmarks against which to judge and rate her worth, success and purpose.

There are other ways to evaluate worth and purpose. For example, Louise has worth and value to herself and her family. A purposeful life may also be defined in non-societal terms, such as having fun, feeling good and bringing cheer to others. These ways are often ignored as important.

Consider a third illustration. Fred is an executive who avoided delegating responsibilities to others, and accordingly, was overloaded with work. The benefits of delegating responsibilities were obvious to Fred. There would be fewer overtime work hours, less stress, and more time spent with his wife and children. Despite these strong reinforcers for change, Fred was still reluctant to delegate. Why? When I asked him what he would lose if he delegated responsibilities to others, Fred hesitatingly replied, "I would feel less needed."

At the office, his advice, counsel and involvement in others' work made Fred feel liked, appreciated and needed. He was dependent upon others' approval for a sense of self-worth. This was identified as a competing reinforcer and part of the problem.

Fred was taught to challenge and dispute his belief that self-worth depended upon others' approval. Once this barrier to change was removed, treatment focused on teaching Fred how to be assertive and effective at work, home and in social settings.

Goals were set and Fred was given homework assignments to put what he had learned into actual behaviors in real settings. Measurements were taken. Fred was asked to record three ratings on a ten-point scale. He rated the effectiveness of his new performance, good feelings, and positive thoughts which included thoughts of self-worth.

These ratings were compared with how Fred rated previous behaviors, feelings and thoughts in similar situations in the past. The change in measurements of rating allowed us to evaluate Fred's progress and the effectiveness of the therapeutic treatment. Data. Data. Data.

In a few sessions our goals were achieved and Fred was delighted with his own sense of accomplishment, effectiveness, and thoughts of self-worth. He was now able to delegate responsibilities without a fear that his self-worth was at risk. There was now more time to spend with his family and to partake in recreational activities. The number of positive reinforcers in Fred's life had increased dramatically. He was both effective and happy at work, at home, and socially.

A final case study illustrates how a competing reinforcer almost sabotaged gains already made in therapy. After the first two hour session, Linda showed remarkable progress. Her Depression Score improved from a 37 indicating severe depression, to a 12 indicating borderline depression. A score of 10 or less is healthy-normal.

As the second session was coming to a close, Linda had a sad face and started to cry. This caught me by surprise since I sensed that we had gained even more ground. When I asked her why she was crying and what was upsetting her, she replied, "I'm afraid I'll hurt my husband."

"What?" I said, and thought to myself, "Where did this come from?"

She repeated,"I'm afraid I'll hurt my husband. I don't want to leave him alone. He needs me. He can't look after himself."

With further probing I realized that Linda's remarkable progress was now being challenged by thoughts of getting better "at what cost". She had not expected recovery to be at her doorstep so quickly. This expectation was probably based on her previous therapies with psychiatrists that lasted for years and went nowhere.

The benefits of getting better were now in conflict with unpleasant things that might happen if she were no longer depressed. "When I'm no longer depressed," she said, "and become a stronger person, I just might leave my husband. But I don't want to hurt him."

"Are there any other costs to getting better?" I enquired.

"Yes", she replied. "I'm afraid that when I'm no longer depressed, things will return to the way they were."

"And how were they?" I asked.

"Friends and especially family used to take advantage of me. They always expected me to solve their problems, and quite often there was nothing I could do. I'm afraid that this will happen again. I'm afraid to say "no" to people. I don't want to hurt their feelings. I don't like disappointing others. I'm afraid of not pleasing them."

Fortunately we were able to identify and remove these competing reinforcers before progress could be sabotaged and derailed.

In the third session, Linda was taught to challenge and dispute her beliefs of worthlessness and thoughts of self-blame. She was then taught behavioral skills of assertiveness.

Between sessions Linda was given homework assignments to demonstrate her assertiveness in specific situations in which she had previously been intimidated. Linda accomplished her tasks with flying colors. She was amazed how well things turned out and felt very proud. I told her that it gets easier with practice.

After three sessions, Linda's Depression Score improved from a 37 indicating severe depression to a 4 indicating no depression. As well, her rating of General Happiness on a ten-point scale improved from a 2 out of 10 to a 10 out of 10. Linda was now on her way to becoming an effective person with power over herself.

Do I really want to go over the hump and get better? Is it worth it? At what cost?

Let's review how a therapist can enhance a client's motivation and efforts to work at getting better.

- First, we discussed the importance of identifying and weakening both the benefits of remaining depressed and the costs of getting better. This should be done in conjunction with efforts to strengthen the benefits of getting better and emphasize the costs of remaining depressed.

  This sounds like a mouthful. For added simplification, please refer to the cost-benefit analysis chart.

- Second, we discussed the monitoring of progress and the keeping of data. Documented progress can be a very strong motivator that enhances efforts toward further progress. It also enhances a client's thoughts of accomplishment and self-worth.

- This brings us to a third point. Clients who perceive themselves as worthless may think that they aren't worth "the effort". We are referring to both the client's efforts and the therapist's efforts. As such thoughts are challenged and disputed, client's efforts toward further improvement will be enhanced and rewarded.

- There is a fourth issue that we have not discussed. If clients perceive their problems as permanent, unchangeable and untreatable, they will exert very little effort to assist the therapist and will give up easily. Thoughts of helplessness and hopelessness are disputed and replaced with an optimism for change. The therapist can tip the motivational balance by demystifying the nature of the problem.

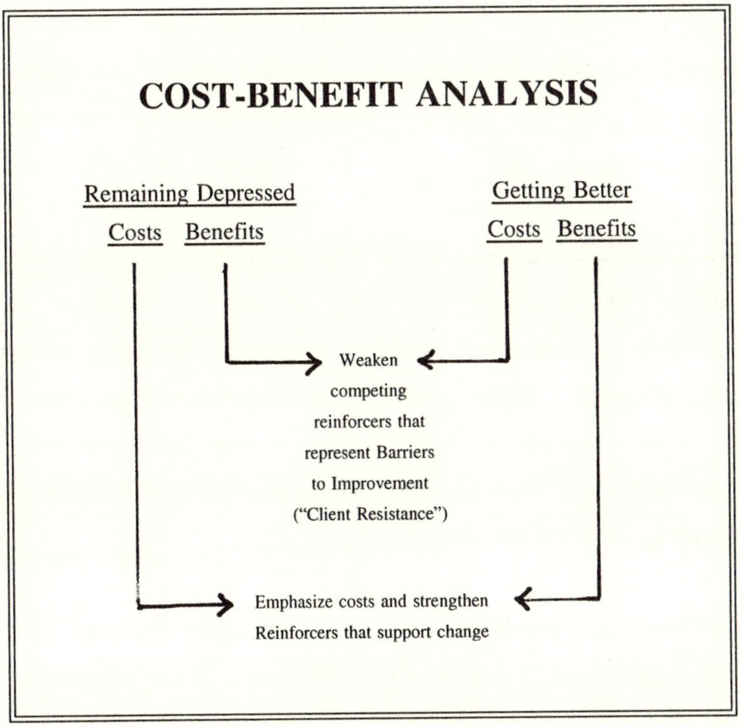

There's a story here. About a year ago I received a phone call from Jane, a prospective client, who asked me if I knew what **dysthymic disorder** was and how to treat it. I said "yes". It is nothing more than psychiatric psycho-babble for depression. Jane told me that she had been diagnosed by a psychiatrist a few years ago as having dysthymic disorder and was unsuccessfully treated by him for about ten months before she quit therapy.

Jane assumed that the diagnostic label must be valid and meaningful since it came from a person of "power and authority". She believed what she was told but knew little about the disorder. What she did know, however, was that treatment was ineffective.

The Diagnostic and Statistical Manual, published by the American Psychiatric Association, is replete with all forms of disorders. There are personality disorders, anxiety disorders, conduct disorders, affective disorders, eating disorders and attention-deficit disorders. While all these disorders suggest a deficiency within the person, they are actually nothing more than behavioral problems that can be swiftly treated by behavioral solutions.

Psychiatry has granted itself the power to label, but unfortunately it can't grant itself the power to effectively treat. Whether two psychiatrists agree or not on a diagnostic label matters little, since neither knows how to effectively treat either disorder. It is a case of labeling without consequences. It means nothing. The emperor is naked.

What Good Is A

Diagnostic Label If It

Doesn't Correspond To

An Effective Treatment?

Diagnostic labeling puts a mystery into the problem. It is couched in psycho-babble, called a disorder or disease, and locates the cause within the person. This often scares and intimidates patients and creates a dependency upon the "emperor" and his apparent wisdoms.

While psychiatry puts the mystery into a problem, it is my task to demystify the nature of the problem. This is done by showing clients how the problem may have been acquired, and how it is presently being sustained by existing reinforcers in the environment. I then proceed to present a rationale for effective treatment toward change.

Once the mystery is removed, the problem is perceived as temporary, changeable and treatable. This offers optimism toward change.

Jane came to see me. Within three sessions her Depression Score improved from severe depression to a healthy-normal.

I want to say a few words about optimism. **Optimism is different than hope**. Hope is always present. It is nothing more than wishful thinking. In therapy, hope represents a desire to get better, but not a willingness to expend effort and work at getting better. We're always hopeful even when we're not optimistic. For example, "I hope I win the lottery, but I'm not optimistic."

Optimism is a statement of probability that something good will happen. It is based on previous evidence and present conditions. In other words, it is a statement that reflects data, and accordingly goes beyond desires and wishes. Clients who perceive the plausibility and optimism of recovery have a greater commitment to work for change. For this reason it becomes important to demystify the nature of the problem, set goals, and collect data.

I cannot emphasize enough how crucial client motivation is to effective therapy. This is the therapist's task. Even good treatment strategies may be derailed without client motivation. It would be like getting on a train that is missing an engine."

Hope Is

Wishful Thinking.

Optimism Is An

Empirical Statement

Of Probability

Based on Data.

CHAPTER **3**

DEPRESSION, MEDICATION AND A BIOCHEMICAL IMBALANCE

"Most of the clients I see, arrive dissatisfied after many years of psychotherapy or after treatment with anti-depressant medications.

The medical establishment treats all psychological-behavioral problems as if they were physical illnesses. They "push" drugs. With hammer in hand, everything is treated as a nail.

Anti-depression drugs are a billion dollar business. Treatment by drugs is so prevalent that many general practitioners no longer refer patients to psychiatrists. Their reasoning is, "Why bother, they're only going to prescribe a drug such as Prozac. I can do that myself and earn extra money."

This present shift to drug treatment by the medical establishment is an implicit acknowledgment that conventional psychiatric therapies do not work. They are ineffective, costly and waste time. The emperor died naked. We just haven't buried him yet.

Let's assume that you are suffering with depression and are told by a physician to take Prozac.

What **assumptions** are being made?

- First, drug treatments assume that a biochemical imbalance is the primary cause of depression.
- Second, the physician is assuming that a biochemical imbalance exists in you.
- Third, the physician is assuming that Prozac will correct that particular imbalance.

All depressions are not accompanied by chemical deficiencies. **Medical practitioners, however, almost never investigate the actual presence of a biochemical imbalance**. In other words, anti-depressant drugs are given to patients to correct a biochemical imbalance without first testing whether or not an imbalance exists. That is the **first act of negligence**.

There is a **second act of negligence**. If Prozac, for example, has been prescribed for your depression, this assumes that the biochemical imbalance is a deficiency of serotonin. Prozac will specifically increase the availability of serotonin. But, what if your depression is caused by a depletion of another chemical such as norepinephrine? If that were the case, then you'd be out of luck. Prozac would be ineffective.

We have raised two negligences. First, Prozac is prescribed without any thought as to whether or not a biochemical imbalance exists at all. Second, whether or not serotonin is the chemical that is deficient. The medical establishment prescribes Prozac with a shot-gun mentality.

Research has associated some depressions with a presence of different biochemical imbalances. There are studies that associate depression with a depletion of serotonin, and there are other studies that associate depression with a depletion of norepinephrine. There are also studies that associate depression with other chemical deficiencies. Without testing, how do we know which chemical is deficient? We don't!

This is an important question to answer since different anti-depressant drugs correct different biochemical imbalances. Prozac, for example, slows down the reabsorption of serotonin into the brain's nerve cells, thereby correcting a depletion of serotonin. On the other hand, tricyclic anti-depressant drugs such as Imipramine inhibit the reabsorption of the chemical norepinephrine, thereby correcting its depletion.

While both drugs are anti-depressants, their effectiveness or ineffectiveness depends upon the existence of a chemical deficiency and upon which chemical is deficient. Identifying the chemical in depletion should determine the type of medication to prescribe. To prescribe an anti-depression drug without this knowledge is a form of negligence that is condoned by the medical establishment.

Serotonin and norepinephrine are neurotransmitters between nerve cells in the brain. Each chemical produces a different type of activity. This is why it is important to know which activity you want to control and which drug can control it. Serotonin is an <u>inhibitor</u>. It reduces activities of nerve cells in the brain, thereby producing a calming effect. Norepinephrine, on the other hand, is an <u>excitator</u>. It increases activities of nerve cells that produce a stimulating effect. For this reason, if you decide to treat depression by medication, it becomes important to know not only if there is a chemical deficiency but which chemical is deficient.

A third act of negligence concerns an absence of systematically monitoring the effectiveness of a drug's treatment. To test for effectiveness, it becomes necessary to take measurements of the same depression symptoms prior to and following the start of drug treatment. Frequent and repeated measurements allow us to monitor any changes in symptoms of depression. If your physician doesn't collect data, I suggest that you do!

We are describing a scientific approach of testing for effectiveness. While it is important, most physicians neglect to perform this aspect of treatment. Always keep in mind, physicians are practitioners and not scientists. At best, they may occasionally ask you how you're feeling. To which you may respond with something like, "I think I'm feeling better but I'm not sure." My advice is to remove the "I think..." and start systematically collecting data.

If you are reluctant to take drugs, but still believe that a biochemical imbalance is the cause of your depression, there is an alternative treatment - **amino acids and supplemental vitamins**.

Let's examine this approach. Prozac corrects a deficiency of serotonin. The same effect can be achieved by ingesting the amino acid tryptophan. Tryptophan naturally converts into serotonin. In other words, both can correct the same chemical deficiency.

Likewise, tricyclics such as Imipramine correct a deficiency of norepinephrine. This same deficiency can be corrected by ingesting the amino acid L-phenylalanine, which naturally converts into norepinephrine.

THREE ACTS OF NEGLIGENCE

(1) Not Testing For The Existence Of A Biochemical Imbalance

(2) No Concern For Which Chemical Is Deficient. Different Drugs Restore Different Chemical Imbalances.

(3) No Systematic Monitoring And Collecting Of Data To Determine If Drug Treatment Is Effective.

If you have not been informed about this alternative treatment, there are two possible answers. First, your physician may not have this knowledge. Second, since amino acids are non-prescription, a shift away from drugs would cost the drug companies and physicians a lot of revenue. You would be visiting doctors fewer times and would be less dependent upon them. This is not something they care to see happen. Think about it."

Someone in the group asks a question. "Dr. Samuel, your comments on negligence make me wonder if I can really trust anybody. It's scary."

Dr. Samuel answers. "**Trust data**."

Another question. "**What kind of tests indicate which chemical is deficient?**"

"An <u>indirect</u> approach to detect depletions of serotonin or norepinephrine or other chemicals is to test for a deficiency of the amino acids that convert into them. This can be tested by a urinary analysis. The test is called a **quantitative urinary amino acid screening test**. For example, a shortage of tryptophan would suggest a depletion of serotonin. A shortage of phenylalanine would suggest a depletion of norepinephrine.

We can also <u>directly</u> test for deficiencies of chemicals using a blood or urine sample. The test is called an **Immuno Radio Assay** (IRA). It tests specifically for one chemical at a time. So, if you suspected a deficiency of serotonin, your hunch could be directly tested."

Another question. "**If the appropriate tests are done on a depressed person, and we find a biochemical imbalance, does that prove that the imbalance caused the depression?**"

Dr. Samuel responds. "It proves nothing. Let's look at the evidence that is available. What we have is the presence of depression and the presence of a biochemical imbalance occurring at the same time. You might guess that the imbalance caused the depression.

Are there any other plausible interpretations? Isn't it plausible that the depression came first and caused the imbalance? This would make a chemical deficiency an effect of depression and not a cause of depression.

Isn't it also plausible that something else caused both the depression and the chemical deficiency? This would make each an effect of another causal factor. In other words, from the evidence available, we can't separate cause from effect in those cases in which a chemical deficiency and depression simultaneously exist.

My position is that both depression and a chemical deficiency are effects of something else that is causing both. That something else is an absence of positive reinforcers. In other words, an absence of positive reinforcers causes depression. Research supports this. As well, an absence of positive reinforcers probably causes a chemical deficiency. We need research in this area.

I'm going to give you a **"quick and easy test" to determine whether the cause is biochemical or environmental**. If the cause is a chemical deficiency and remains uncorrected, then the depression will also remain. It will remain even when the depressed person is in an environment that is very positively reinforcing.

On the other hand, if changes in a reinforcing environment alter behaviors, moods and thoughts in a positive direction, you will then know that the cause is not a chemical deficiency. It is a behavioral problem that is caused by an absence of positive reinforcers."

If A Biochemical Imbalance Is The Cause, Depression Will Remain Despite Changes In A Reinforcing Environment.

If Behaviors, Moods And Thoughts Improve In A Reinforcing Environment, Then The Cause Is Not A Chemical Deficiency.

Lisa ponders what was said. "That's brilliant and yet so simple. I'll bet there are so many depressed people who are being mistreated with medication."

"Whatever chemical reactions occur in the brain, they are **part of a "causal chain"**. They do not initiate anything on their own. This "internal part " of a causal chain bridges the gap between reinforcers in the environment and behaviors, moods and thoughts. In other words, it bridges input and output.

Anti-depressant drugs merely tap into part of that causal chain. They may correct a chemical depletion and provide temporary relief for as long as the medication is present. This is the reason some physicians recommend permanently maintaining patients on anti-depressant medication.

It is not uncommon for patients to have relapses of depression when medication is discontinued. This is not surprising as long as the patient's environment remains non-reinforcing. In other words, depression remains a permanent threat until the primary cause has been dealt with.

CAUSAL CHAIN

(B)
INTERNAL PART OF
A CAUSAL CHAIN

(A)
INPUT

(C)
OUTPUT

chemicals between
nerve cells

Absence of Positive Reinforcers →

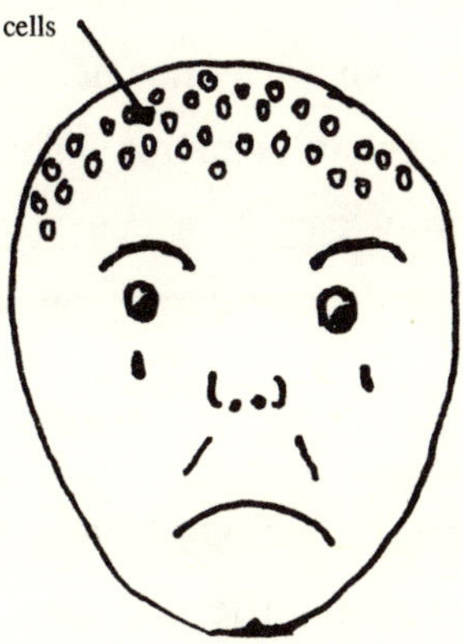

→ Dysfunctional Behaviors, Bad Moods, Negative Thoughts

As you've gathered, my approach is to analyze relationships between behaviors and reinforcers in the environment. This is called a **Behavioral Analysis**.

Although it is beyond challenge, it does not proclaim that a behavioral explanation is complete. Actually any account of behavior is always incomplete. For example, if we added a neurological explanation to account for behavioral processes, would the account then be complete? No. It might then be argued that we must explain the neurological findings by studying cell biology. And to explain cell biology we must study biochemistry. And to explain biochemistry we must study chemistry and physics. And finally to explain this, we must study subatomic particles. In other words, an explanation or understanding of behavior is never complete. Behavior is merely studied at different levels.

A main point I want to address is that a Behavioral Analysis is faultless. It stands on its own. It is not necessary to refer to the nervous system in order to explain behavior. The nervous system is a causal captive that is merely part of a causal chain. It mediates between what is fed into it and what comes out of it, and does not initiate activity on its own.

Research in neurology, biology, biochemistry, etc., may provide valuable information about different parts of the causal chain. Such information, however, can never cast doubt on the validity of behavioral processes or on any consistent relationship established between behaviors and reinforcers. As a matter of fact, any new information acquired in these other sciences must be validated against changes in behavior.

A behavioral account is sufficient to explain behaviors and to develop effective treatment strategies for behavioral changes."

Information In Neurology, Biochemistry, etc., Can Never Cast Doubt On The Validity Of Behavioral Principles.

Behavioral Principles Stand On Their Own.

CHAPTER **4**

UNDERSTANDING, USE AND APPLICATION OF POSITIVE REINFORCEMENT

"Before we proceed, it is important to establish a working knowledge and understanding of the concept of positive reinforcement and the role it plays in our lives.

For our purposes, we will define a **positive reinforcer** as any stimulus, event, activity or experience that is satisfying enough to strengthen the behavior that produced it. Because we want to see these satisfying experiences recur, we will repeat those behaviors that produced them. The satisfying nature of these experiences are good feelings and positive thoughts. The behaviors that produced them may be called **effective behaviors**.

There are different groupings of positive reinforcers.

Some positive reinforcers are naturally and genetically programed at birth. These reinforcers belong to all members of our species without any prior learning. Since their reinforcing powers are not conditional upon prior learning, they are called **unconditional reinforcers**. This list includes: food, water, sexual stimulation, air, rest after activity, activity after rest and a comfortable range of temperatures.

A much larger list of positive reinforcers are called **conditioned reinforcers**. They are not given at birth but have acquired their reinforcing power by prior learning and associations. Their reinforcing power is conditional upon past associations and prior learning. These reinforcers do not belong to all members of a species but are idiosyncratic to particular individuals.

A powerful class of conditional reinforcers are **verbal**. They include "right", "correct", "good", forms of attention and approval. These reinforcers are mediated by other persons and are maintained by our society. We will work for them and their occurrence can strengthen behaviors that produce them.

In summary, a positive reinforcer is defined by:

- (a) its impact on behaviors that produced it, and

- (b) good feelings and positive thoughts that accompanied and characterized the satisfying nature of the experience.

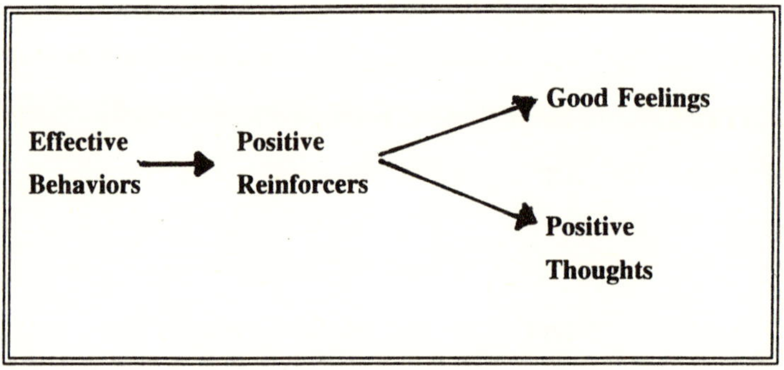

A primary goal of therapy is to increase, on a daily basis, the **density of positive reinforcers** in our lives. This will not only prevent a depression from occurring, but will break an existing depression.

A therapist can teach you to recognize your personal positive reinforcers and how to connect with them through effective behaviors. Such application and use of effective behaviors and positive reinforcers will dramatically change your life and get it back on a healthy track.

When suffering with depression, there is not only an absence of positive reinforcers but also an absence of behaviors that were previously sustained by those reinforcers. These losses are often dwelled upon and distract us from initiating effective behaviors to regain positive reinforcers from either old or new sources. If some sources are blocked, positive reinforcement may be obtained from other sources.

While in the grip of depression, it becomes very difficult to connect with positive reinforcers. There may be a lack of motivation to increase effective behaviors. There may also be a lack of awareness as to what behaviors are actually effective.

In the midst of depression we don't believe that anything can or will make a difference. Sometimes we can't even remember what it feels like not to be depressed.

Depression is like living in a world of which we are not a part. There is an emptiness inside. There is a feeling that we are enclosed within a thin film that prevents connection to the world around us. It hurts and it is debilitating. While we may observe positive reinforcers work for others, they don't work for us. We are unable to penetrate that thin film and connect with our reinforcers. Any attempts to do so are futile and unproductive. So we give up. We sulk. We surrender life. We become "the living dead". We become Zombies.

During depression, we not only avoid what makes us feel bad, but we also ignore what makes us feel good. Any optimism for change is lost.

A therapist-coach can remind us of previous positive reinforcers and guide us through effective behaviors to connect with those reinforcers.

Much of depression centers around thoughts of **helplessness** to alter an absence of positive reinforcers. Depression also centers around thoughts of **hopelessness** that this void or absence is permanent, unchangeable and untreatable.

These thoughts are learned. There is a perception of being unable to control the positive reinforcers in one's life. The opposite of helplessness is **mastery**, in which one perceives that our own behaviors are responsible for positive reinforcers.

We often perceive the cause of helplessness and depression to be something <u>internal</u>. Once an internal cause is perceived, the problem is accepted as unchangeable and it becomes easier to give up and not try. Such surrendering diminishes opportunities for positive reinforcement and simultaneously enhances self-blame for being an inadequate person.

Research with animals and humans has demonstrated how pre-arranged experiences of failure and ineffectiveness can lead to a learning of helplessness. For example, animals were placed in traumatic situations that were inescapable. Children were given problems to solve that were unsolvable. Following these experiences of ineffectiveness and failure, the studies indicated that motivation and efforts to succeed in new situations were short-lived.

A sense of helplessness quickly generalized to new and different situations. There was a learned expectation that performances would be futile and ineffective.

In other words, a past history of ineffective performances led to pessimistic expectations for further ineffectiveness. There was a perceived lack of control over positive reinforcers. Such a lack of control is often attributed to an internal trait within the person, implying that ineffectiveness and incompetence come from within.

What is notably significant is not only an **absence of positive reinforcers**, but a perceived **absence of control over positive reinforcers**.

In therapy, it becomes crucial to focus on creating a history of effective behaviors that lead to satisfying experiences. To facilitate this outcome, it is extremely valuable to have a knowledge of the relationship between personal positive reinforcers and the effective behaviors that can produce them. This applies not only to individuals but also to couples.

While it is a client's responsibility to initiate effective action and to incorporate daily reinforcers into his/her life, it is a therapist's responsibility to motivate clients and teach and guide effective behaviors toward positive reinforcers.

Clients may be guided to connect and get in touch with positive reinforcers that previously were accompanied by good feelings and positive thoughts.

- First, they are asked to list **activities**, events and experiences in the past that were accompanied by good feelings and positive thoughts. These are previous experiences that they enjoyed and found satisfying.

  Clients are encouraged to incorporate some of these positive reinforcers on a regular, routine basis, whether it be daily, weekly, monthly, etc.

- Second, clients are asked to list **persons** who have previously encouraged, reinforced and appreciated behaviors the client expresses and attributes that he/she possesses.

Seek these persons out. They are <u>sources</u> of positive reinforcement for you. For example, persons who laugh at your jokes, are attentive, enjoy your company, etc. This characterizes a reinforcing environment for you.

- Third, clients are asked to start attending to, and **becoming aware of current positive reinforcers**. These reinforcers are to be listed.

Many of these reinforcers may have previously been taken for granted. They might have remained unrecognized as sources of good feelings and positive thoughts until verbalized and made explicit. For example, "I've got my health", "I've got a job", "I just ate a good meal", "I laughed", "My car works", etc.

Clients may also <u>contrast</u> these taken for granted positive reinforcers with imagined thoughts of what things would be like if these satisfying events were absent.

- Fourth, clients are asked to list their own **personal attributes and expressed behaviors that have been and are reinforcing to other persons**.

This emphasizes the client's valuable capacity as a provider of positive reinforcement to other persons, and as a contributor to their good feelings and positive thoughts. Such knowledge of "giving and contributing" can be positively reinforcing to clients.

- Fifth, to increase the frequency of positive reinforcers received, clients are encouraged to **provide more positive reinforcement to other persons**. This enhances the probability of receiving positive reenforcement from others. Those who give, get!

It is not unusual for clients to be unaware that their reactions and comments have an impact on another person's performance, feelings and thoughts. Although they may perceive themselves as being ineffective and not affecting others, they can often be a powerful source of positive reinforcers.

- Sixth, sometimes opportunities for positive reinforcers are <u>only</u> able to occur following an earlier occurrence of a traumatic event. The trauma and subsequent "pain" are, at times, a "blessing in disguise", even though they are not recognized as such when trauma strikes. For example, following rejection and break-up of an unhappy relationship, Arlene went through a depression until she actively sought a suitable partner with whom she happily shared love and life. Positive reinforcement was being reciprocated.

Arlene's happy situation can be contrasted to a miserable existence that would have been perpetuated if she had not suffered a traumatic experience of rejection, divorce and change.

In other words, quite often when unpleasant traumatic things happen to us, we can ask ourselves two questions: (a) Would it really be better to remain in that unpleasant situation? and (b) What positive things can *now* emerge? Consider a previous "hurt" as an *opportunity* for positive change and improvement of one's lifestyle. Be optimistic.

A powerful way to break a depression is to establish a reinforcing environment and to create effective behaviors that produce positive reinforcers.

Clients are encouraged to build up an arsenal of positive reinforcers and effective behaviors that are ready for use. Part of the arsenal includes positive reinforcers that are incorporated into *daily* living. Other reinforcers may be of a longer-term nature and require planning. Planned activities enable us to frequently anticipate the joys we will experience prior to their occurrence.

Even when depressed, the resources for change are still available. The power is *always* yours to alter your environment and to change your behaviors toward effectiveness. Once these conditions are set up by you, positive reinforcers in the environment will have a positive impact on your behaviors, feelings and thoughts.

Become an active agent of effectiveness and positive reinforcement. Start now! It's never too late. Good feelings and positive thoughts are yours for the making."

CHAPTER 5

Feelings, Moods and Emotions

"Why do people have good or bad feelings? Why do people have positive or negative thoughts? Feelings and thoughts are effects or by-products of reinforcers. They are temporary and will change as reinforcers in the environment change. Although experienced as private events, make no mistake, they are caused by reinforcers.

When we feel good, we are not feeling goodness per se, but are feeling good about something. That something is a positive reinforcer. We experience and feel the effects of reinforcers. Again, things feel good because they are positively reinforcing. Think of the times that you've had good feelings and positive thoughts. Didn't they always follow something enjoyable? For example, sex, accomplishments, receiving a smile, etc.

Feelings and Thoughts are Effects or By-Products of Reinforcers.

Let's play emotional trivia. You give me the name of an emotion and let's see if I can define it as an effect of a reinforcer."

"Anger."

"Anger results from a discontinuation of a positive reinforcer."

"Joy."

"Joy may be caused by the presentation of a positive reinforcer, especially following a period of being without."

"Grief."

"Grief may be caused by the loss of a positively reinforcing person."

"Anxiety."

"Anxiety may be caused by the presentation of a negative reinforcer. An escape from this will provide relief."

"Loneliness."

"Loneliness may be caused by a prolonged absence of certain people whom we associate with positive reinforcement. If they are family members then the emotion is homesickness."

"Stress. I'm going through a lot of stress at work. I'm burning out."

"Yes, I understand. You're doing a lot of work and are getting very few positive reinforcers for your performance. You're not getting enough reinforcers to sustain your performance, and so you want to give up. More specifically, there is a very large ratio of performances per each positive reinforcer you get. What do you think?"

"Ya, that's it all right. I never thought of it in those terms. Makes sense now."

"In the lab," Dr. Samuel continues, "this is called **'ratio strain'**. Ratio strain occurs when you must put forth much work and get little in return. The ratio itself is very traumatic and can produce an avoidance of work as well as "down" feelings and thoughts of inadequacy, incompetence, lack of control, etc. These are effects or by-products of this schedule of reinforcement.

A Very Large Ratio of Performances Per Positive Reinforcement Received Can Produce Stress and Burnout in the Workplace.

There is a very optimistic implication to all of this. Feelings are not something that come from within or just happen to you. As by-products of reinforcers we have some control in modifying our moods. We can seek out or create environments that are positively reinforcing. Remember, you are not a victim of your moods. Do something about it!

I think it is important to elaborate on exactly what effects are directly produced by reinforcers. These effects occur simultaneously. We're going to focus on **physiological effects and behavioral effects**.

Let's examine some of the physiological effects that occur when having a traumatic experience. This is often labeled as **anxiety**.

First, your pulse and heart rate are higher which increases circulation of blood. Second, your breathing quickens. This expands the surface of the lungs which increases the supply of oxygen into the blood. Third, the adrenal glands secrete more adrenalin which acts on the liver to release sugar into the blood. The result of all this is that **we are experiencing an increased supply of oxygen and sugar in the blood that is rapidly being circulated.**

Simultaneously we may attempt to avoid or escape from such a traumatic experience. This is the behavioral effect.

What happens when a traumatic experience is perceived as "very" traumatic, frightening or painful? The physiological effects become very heightened and intense, and may overwhelm and suppress the behavioral effects of escape and avoidance. If intense enough, they may even suppress all existing behaviors, leaving us immobilized. We are familiar with statements such as, "I was so frightened I couldn't move", or "I was paralyzed with fright", or "He was frightened to death" (heart attack), or "I was speechless with rage".

In other words, what we have described is an **interaction between physiological effects and behavioral effects**.

This interaction has important implications for an understanding and treatment of **anxiety** and **panic attacks**. If we are able to escape from a traumatic experience, then the intensity of physiological effects are dampened, feelings of anxiety are reduced, and relief is provided. However, and this is most important, when we perceive that we cannot avoid or escape from a traumatic event, a state of high anxiety or panic may result. Why? First, the traumatic event continues. Second, the event continues to produce intense physiological effects. Third, these effects cannot be stopped by escape. There is no perceived escape or solution to the problem.

High anxiety and panic may be compounded even further by thoughts of helplessness and even hopelessness. There is a perception of an inadequacy to escape and a lack of control. Not only can we not control what is happening to us in our lives, but we also feel an inability to control the panic itself. The heightened physiological effect is often interpreted as life-threatening.

Fortunately for us, environmental distractions usually weaken the physiological intensity, making panic attacks a short-lived experience. Relaxation techniques serve the same function. They distract and provide only temporary relief.

INTERACTION EFFECT

Traumatic Events/Cues
Simultaneously Produce

Physiological Effects

Behavioral Effects
e.g., Escape, Avoidance

(A) If escape occurs, a lid is kept on the physiological effect.

escape behavior
places a lid
==== on physiological
↑ effects

(B) If there is no perceived escape, then the physiological effect may continue unabated, resulting in a panic attack.

↑
↑ Physiological Effects
↑ continue unabated

Martha is someone who had panic attacks almost daily. She had recently been rejected by her boyfriend, was unemployed, and seemed not to be in control of much in her life. She saw herself as a hang-nail on the fickle finger of fate. And to top that off, she was now having panic attacks.

Martha could not identify any specific situation with the attacks and did not know what caused them. "They seem to come out of nowhere at any time and any place." This is not an unusual answer for someone suffering with panic attacks.

Pertinent to our discussion, Martha perceived a lack of control over the positive reinforcers in her life and over the panic attacks. Everything bad was happening to her. She perceived no control and no escape or solution to her problems. Her behaviors were ineffective.

Ineffective performances lead to negative reinforcers or an absence of positive reinforcers. The by-products of this are feelings of anxiety and thoughts of inadequacy, low self-worth, helplessness and lack of control. If no escape or solution is perceived, panic attacks may follow.

Within this framework, I saw a way to rid Martha of her panic attacks. I taught Martha how to be effective. Effective behaviors led to positive reinforcers. The by-products of positive reinforcers are good feelings, certainly no anxiety, and thoughts of adequacy, accomplishment, self-worth, mastery and control. As Martha gained control over positive reinforcers in her life, the panic attacks disappeared."

EFFECTIVE/INEFFECTIVE BEHAVIORS AS RELATED TO PANIC/NO PANIC

A. **Ineffective Behaviors** → Negative Reinforcers or an Absence of Positive Reinforcers → (a) Feelings of Anxiety and (b) Thoughts of No Control, No Escape and No Solutions → **PANIC**

B. **Effective Behaviors** → Positive Reinforcers → (a) "Up" Feelings and (b) Thoughts of Accomplishment, Mastery, Self-Worth and Control → **NO PANIC**

Someone in the group comments. "I'm a nervous person. I'm always somewhat anxious and don't know why. Certain things, people, activities, the way I'm spoken to at times, can really make me anxious. It's everyday occurrences that make me anxious. Do you have any explanation for that?"

Dr. Samuel reflects for a moment, then responds, "Yes I do. The answer lies in how the past is linked to the present. Let me explain. In the past, perhaps during childhood, some of the things you did may have been followed by negative reinforcers. These were traumatic experiences for you, and they were accompanied by physiological effects, feelings of anxiety and thoughts of incompetence, worthlessness, helplessness, etc. For example, you may have failed an exam and were told by your teacher or parent that you are dumb and won't amount to a hill of beans. You may have been awkward in dating and had embarrassing moments that others kept reminding you of. You may have bungled many assignments or tasks given to you. You may have been yelled at repeatedly by angry parents and made to think that you are incompetent and stupid. The list goes on. This is the baggage you carry into adulthood.

You may have been too young to question authority figures at that time. You were probably also too young to leave the situation. In other words, you had to tolerate it.

You never learned to dispute the nonsense you were fed. It was accepted as factual. As long as you continue to believe it, in the present, you will continue to have problems.

These early traumatic experiences took place in the presence of **internal cues** such as physiological effects, bodily and muscle movements. They also took place in the presence of **external cues** such as certain sights, smells, sounds, tones of voice, etc. By an <u>association</u> with early traumatic experiences, these neutral things have taken on power to produce in the present, very similar effects that we experienced in the past.

So, in the present, when we encounter these cues, we may re-experience feelings of anxiety and thoughts of incompetence, failure, helplessness, lack of control. These are feelings and thoughts similar to what we experienced in the past. For example, a re-experience may be triggered by the tone of someone's voice, a disapproving other, any minor mistake you might make, someone's appearance, a room that looks similar to that in your old house, etc.

Just as we tried to escape from or avoid earlier traumatic experiences, we also, in the present, attempt to escape from or avoid any cues that are associated with past trauma. Does that answer your question?"

"Yes, thank you. It also helps me understand why I avoid certain persons and activities."

Dr. Samuel continues. "A few more comments on **avoidance**. We do not avoid situations because we expect something bad to happen. Expectations do not cause or explain avoidance. Fears, anxieties and negative expectations are effects or by-products of traumatic experiences in the past.

In the short-term, avoidance provides relief and temporary control. In the longer-term, however, that same avoidance will maintain feelings of anxiety and thoughts of inadequacy, cowardice, helplessness and low self-worth. In other words, avoidance provides a short-term gain at the expense of long-term pain.

Knowledge, awareness or "insight" about the linkage between internal/external associative cues and past traumas, is of little therapeutic value by itself. This knowledge does, however, provide a rationale for effective treatments.

In therapy it becomes necessary to **neutralize these cues associated with past trauma**.

This can be accomplished by:

- First showing clients how to **dispute the correctness and attached meaning of negative beliefs** that are triggered by associative cues. In other words, to dispute the nonsense that has been believed and accepted as valid for so many years. This includes thoughts of worthlessness, failure, inadequacy, etc.

- Second, clients are taught **how to be presently effective** in situations that previously generated feelings of anxiety and self-depreciating thoughts."

CHAPTER 6

Confusion Between Causes and Effects

"Since we experience feelings and thoughts privately, it is not unusual to confuse their source of origin. They don't originate within us and don't cause anything. They are effects of reinforcers in the environment. It is these effects that we experience.

Confusion between cause and effect is illustrated in statements such as, "Persons who feel good, do good work." This statement implies that feelings cause good performance. It is incorrect. "Persons who do good work, feel good." What feels good is the accomplishment of a good performance. What may also feel good are praise, money, and thoughts of control and mastery that follow a good performance.

Conventional therapies mistakenly treat feelings and thoughts as internal causes of behaviors. They may spend years exploring feelings and thoughts about problems, life, etc. "Well, how do you feel about that?" Their mistaken hope is that changes in behavior will emerge if therapy can only get clients to change their feelings about things. It doesn't work.

If you want to change feelings and thoughts you must first change behaviors.

A change in feelings and thoughts will follow. There is an abundance of research on changing attitudes that supports this one-way direction of change.

There are also therapies that strive for "insight". "If we can only get the client to see and understand that such and such events in the past are causing present problems..." This assumes that once the client has such "insight", he will abandon his self-defeating habits, choose a better path, and emerge as a new person. This is nonsense and it doesn't work.

It isn't a lack of "insight" that keeps us depressed, anxious, having low self-esteem, etc. It is ineffective behaviors and present environmental influences.

Some therapists argue that thoughts cause feelings. This is the position of cognitive-behavioral and rational-emotive therapies. But where do thoughts come from? This approach fails to deal with the cause of thoughts. You already know the answer. Thoughts and feelings are effects of reinforcers.

Conventional therapists focus on the person and look for causes within. "Get in touch with your inner feelings and thoughts." "Embrace the child within you." "Confront the devil within you." "Get to know yourself better." These phrases may sound comforting to hear, but they leave you stranded without a plan of action for change. They are meaningless psycho-babble used to dignify ignorance.

By focusing on deficiencies within the person, most therapies ignore the real causes. They ignore reinforcers that cause and sustain habits.

To really know yourself, don't look within. Know your behaviors, know your environments and their reinforcers. And know the relationship between your behaviors and reinforcers.

You will then know how your feelings, thoughts, expectations, fears and personality have been acquired and how they are presently being sustained. You will also know how to implement changes. This is knowledge about your "self" that is truly worth having. Anything else is psycho-babble.

Let's examine some **confusions between cause and effect**.

Last year I received a phone call from Peter, a prospective client, who asked me if I could help him overcome his anxiety. Peter was scheduled to give a presentation in five weeks in front of a large audience. He told me that last time he spoke to a large group he felt so anxious that he stuttered and spoke poorly. "It was a disaster," he said.

Peter's comments imply that anxiety caused his poor speaking performance. This is incorrect. Anxiety is not a cause. It is an effect of negative reinforcers. This was explained to Peter in my office a few days later.

In the past, Peter's verbal performances were probably met with inattention, criticism and disapproval. This could have been story-telling, joke-telling, or just having no one pay attention while talking. The by-products of these negative reinforcers were feelings of anxiety and thoughts of inadequacy, incompetence and worthlessness. Similar feelings and thoughts resurfaced in the present now that Peter had to make a verbal presentation. The anxiety is an effect of negative reinforcers that were brought on by poor performances in the past.

We have turned the problem on its head. It is a behavioral problem that requires a behavioral solution. Since poor performances in the past caused anxiety, the primary focus of treatment is to improve performance in the present within an environment that is positively reinforcing. This was done in the office. Peter repeatedly practiced his speech. First in front of me. Then in front of two persons, four persons and six persons. We also varied the distance between Peter and the audience. This allowed Peter to practice speaking loudly in front of a small group.

As Peter's performance improved, his anxiety diminished. Needless to say, his major presentation went quite well. After his speech, he called to tell me that he actually enjoyed himself and had volunteered to speak again.

What happened? Peter learned effective behaviors that produced positive reinforcers. The by-products of which are good feelings and thoughts of accomplishment, competence, mastery and self-worth. No anxiety.

Many "problems" encountered in therapy, that appear to be inadequacies within the person, are actually behavioral problems. The list is long. It includes personality problems, unhappiness, depression, anxiety, stress, low self-esteem, pessimism and many others.

Just the other day I heard someone remark, "He's so pessimistic, no wonder he's depressed." This implies that pessimism causes depression. It doesn't. It causes nothing. Both pessimism and depression are effects. Pessimism may be an effect of repeated failures in the past. A lack of effectiveness and a lack of control over positive reinforcers in the past has led to pessimistic expectations in the present.

There are three components to effective treatment of these problems:

- First, to teach clients to dispute beliefs of failure, low self-worth, etc.

- Second, to identify and eliminate ineffective behaviors that produce negative reinforcers.

- Third, to teach effective behaviors in specific situations that produce positive reinforcers.

It is not uncommon to explain behaviors by looking for the cause within the person. This happens when we fail to separate our "self" from our behaviors. Sometimes we attempt to legitimize an "inner force" by labeling it with terms such as "self-discipline", "will power" and "self-control". We want to give credit to something within us if it is a good behavior, and attribute blame if it is a bad behavior.

This implies that there are internal forces that are responsible for our behaviors. It is as if these inner forces have "free will" and can choose to behave as they please, irrespective of any influence by reinforcers in the environment. This is nonsense. Behavioral laws exist and are unchangeable. They describe cause-effect relationships between behaviors and their reinforcers. Whether you are aware or not aware of behavioral laws, they still operate. Whether you believe or don't believe in so-called "free will" and "inner forces", behavioral laws still operate.

There is a story in Greek mythology that is pertinent to the issue of inner causes. It is Homer's tale of "Odysseus and the Sirens". The tale seems to challenge the mistaken belief that an "inner strength" can resist the temptations of reinforcers in the environment.

The Sirens were enchantresses who lived on an island surrounded by treacherous rocks. Their sweet and inviting songs lured sailors toward the island and to destruction. Having been forewarned of this danger, Odysseus ordered his shipmates to plug their ears with wax so they could not hear the enticing sounds. Odysseus also gave orders that he be securely tied to the mast, so that he might hear but be unable to react.

The point of interest is how Odysseus dealt with temptation. He did not say "Men, we must exert self-discipline, will power and self-control". Instead, he re-arranged the environment to secure the safety of his ship and crew. Odysseus acted wisely, taking behavioral laws into account. He realized the powers of a reinforcing environment, and took behavioral measures to obstruct their influence. **Control of behaviors lies in the environment and not within the person**."

Someone in the group raised an interesting issue. "Dr. Samuel, if our behaviors are controlled by reinforcers and not by an internal force within us, then **are we responsible for our actions**?"

Dr. Samuel smiles. "You've raised an issue that requires further clarification. Since behaviors are controlled by reinforcers in the environment, we are not responsible for our actions. However, in opposition to this position, it has been argued that we have choices and are responsible for our choices. Therefore, we are responsible for our actions. My rebuttal to that is as follows: Yes, we have choices, but any particular choice we make is determined by the strength of reinforcers.

Perhaps the issue of responsibility has been clouded by a confusion between

(a) being responsible and

(b) being <u>held</u> responsible by others.

This is an important distinction. In other words, while not responsible for our actions, we may, nevertheless, be held responsible by others or society for not following prescribed rules of conduct that have been imposed upon us.

As you can see, these are really two separate issues, and not opposing sides to a single issue. One issue is whether behavior operates according to the laws of reinforcement. The answer is a resounding "Yes". The other issue examines responsibility from a societal, moral, and ethical perspective. It must take into account societal power, the making of laws and their enforcement."

CHAPTER **7**

Separating Your "Self" From Your Mistakes

"When you screw up, do you perceive an ineffective **person** or ineffective **behaviors**?"

Someone answers, "It's both. It's ineffective behavior that comes from an ineffective person."

Dr. Samuel responds. "You are confusing 'self' with your performance. They are not the same. Whatever the screw up, it is a behavior and is specific to a situation. It is also a very small proportion of your total behaviors in any one day. Yet, it is not unusual to generalize from a few incompetent behaviors to a judgment and rating of a whole person. The latter would require an evaluation of "all" behaviors. Were "all" of your behaviors ineffective and dissatisfying? Of course not. They were specific behaviors in specific situations that were rated against specific criteria.

When person and behavior are seen as inseparable, an ineffective or inadequate performance is considered to be the same as an inadequate person. We infer the cause of this inadequacy to be within us. This leads to a judgment and rating of the "self". It is followed by self-criticism, self-blame and guilt.

In other words, we treat our "self" harshly based upon our performances. Thoughts of inadequacy become thoughts of worthlessness. Self-blame and guilt often occur without forgiveness. This can lead to self-dislike and even self-hatred.

The root of such negative self-treatment is an inability to separate person and behavior. Self-evaluation is conditional upon evaluation of our conduct. A prerequisite to unconditional self-acceptance is a separation of person and behavior.

SEPARATION BETWEEN PERSON AND BEHAVIOR

Perceived as Separate

Person	Behavior
↓	↓
Self-Acceptance (Person is a non-issue)	Improve Behaviors

Perceived as Inseparable

Person-Behavior

↓

Inadequacy Within Me

↓

Self-Blame and Guilt

Even when we don't unconditionally accept our "self", we desire and often demand that others unconditionally accept us. In other words, **even when we don't separate person and behavior for ourselves, we expect and demand that others do it for us**. We demand that they do for us what we haven't done for ourselves. We expect others to unconditionally accept us regardless of our misconducts, imperfections and human fallibilities. These are fairy tale expectations, and when violated, we are disappointed, angry and have "hurt feelings".

This is a very interesting paradox. There is a double standard for how we treat ourselves versus how we think others "should" treat us, especially spouses.

How many of you believe in **"unconditional love"**? Most hands are raised. Is that wishful thinking or does it exist? It does exist but is not found very often between spouses. This is evident by the high rate of divorce. Love from a spouse is usually conditional upon the other's performance and conduct. To expect or demand more, makes us vulnerable to "hurt feelings".

Unconditional love most probably exists in the love that parents have for their children. While they may criticize behaviors, parents continue to accept and love the person unconditionally. Why is this so? A plausible explanation may be found in a separation between person and behavior. Parents have a long history of separating the child as person from the child's behaviors. This separation begins at birth. In early childhood, separation is easy. Not many persons would blame a child for misbehaviors. Separation is then more easily extended into adolescence and adulthood.

Both unconditional love and self-acceptance require a separation of person and behavior.

"Expressed love" from others is usually conditional upon our behaviors. It is fleeting and temporary. We may have received letters or cards that expressed an "undying love". "I'll love you forever", or "To the love of my life". Don't mistake conditional and temporary love for unconditional love. Don't get caught in fairy tale expectations based on how you think things "ought to be" or "want them to be".

The only security that you can count on throughout your life is self-acceptance. But before this can be achieved, you must learn to separate your "self" from your behaviors.

Let's review the consequences of <u>not</u> separating person and behavior.

- First, perceiving inseparableness results in a <u>rating of the "self"</u>. This can lead to self-blame, guilt, shame, embarrassment, etc.

- Second, perceived inseparableness results in <u>inferences about internal causes</u> of behavior. This leads to a perception of "problems" as permanent and as cutting across all situations. Such a perception offers little optimism for change and encourages a tendency to give up easily when things aren't going well.

On the other hand, **if we separate person and behavior**,

- first, we have no data upon which to evaluate the "self". Self-rating becomes a non-issue, as do self-blame, guilt, etc. This is self-acceptance. It is unconditional acceptance. It is not the same as self-love or self-like. It merely means that self-rating or self-evaluation is a non-issue.

- Second, any setbacks and failures are perceived as ineffective behaviors that are specific to certain situations. They are perceived as temporary and as changeable with effort and practice. This offers optimism and a readiness to persevere.

A Prerequisite for Self-Acceptance is a Separation of Person and Behavior.

With Separation:

(a) Self-Rating Becomes a Non-Issue.

(b) Focus Entirely on Improving Performances.

Would you believe that Michael Jordan, a super-star NBA player, did not make his high school basketball team? Mr. Jordan could have attributed his mediocre performance to an internal inadequacy that was unchangeable. Instead, he focused on improving his performance. It was perceived as a behavioral problem that required much effort, practice and learning of new skills. This does not imply that effort and perseverance guarantee success. They do not.

But they do enhance the probability of succeeding in many endeavors.

Leon Uris, famous author of "Exodus", is another example of success despite previous failures. Mr. Uris failed English literature three times in high school. Yet, he persevered to success.

Setbacks and failures are an inevitable part of life. How we deal with them is most important.

Here are some **guidelines**:

- First, separate person and behavior. Don't waste time and energy on self-rating. Focus entirely on improving performances. As your behaviors become effective, they will be accompanied by good feelings and thoughts of accomplishment and self-worth.

- Second, if at times you forget to separate person and behavior, you may experience thoughts of inadequacy, self-blame, guilt and low self-worth. At such times, challenge and dispute these self-ratings on two levels: (a) Dispute their empirical correctness by seeking out evidence that proves them false, or at least creates doubt about their validity. (b) Challenge negative meanings and interpretations that you are attaching to setbacks. The meaning may come from underlying assumptions that you are holding about self-worth, the human condition, and the way you think things "should be". Challenge the validity and legitimacy of these assumptions."

Someone asks, "I understand how it can be harmful to attribute "failure" to internal causes, but what's so bad about attributing "success" to internal causes?"

Dr. Samuel ponders the question and responds. "It would certainly boost your self-esteem but it probably isn't sustainable. Let me explain. It's a bad habit that sets up a vulnerability. It's hard to make internal attributions for success only, and not for failure. However, if you can do it, that's great. A safer position is to always separate person and behavior."

Another question from the group. "How come some people separate person and behavior, and others don't?"

Dr. Samuel answers. "Focusing on behavior must have been reinforced in the past. But "why" is not important. What is important is that those who have not learned to separate person and behavior can learn to do so "now"! They can learn to abandon self-evaluations and ratings and focus on improving performance.

It is interesting how our language lends itself to a shift from an evaluation of behavior to an evaluation of the person. I'll explain this in terms of a "**progression**". Let's examine this progression as it applies to "incompetence": (A) "Tom performed incompetently on the test." → (B) "Tom is an incompetent person." → (C) "Tom has a lot of incompetence."

In the first statement, "incompetently" is an <u>adverb</u> that describes Tom's behavior in a specific situation. Now the confusion begins. In the second statement, we readily shift from an adverb that describes behavior to an <u>adjective</u> that describes and characterizes Tom. We have created a personality trait to explain Tom's behavior in "any" situation. Some might say that he has a personality problem that requires years of psychotherapy. While others might assume that Tom was born that way.

In the final stage of the progression we shift from an adjective that characterizes a person to a <u>noun</u>. In other words, we infer that there is some "thing" within Tom to account for his behavior. It is "incompetence".

PROGRESSION OF AN EXPLANATION

(A) An Adverb That Correctly Describes Behavior.

e.g., He performed "incompetently" on the test.

↓

(B) An Adjective That Describes a Person.

e.g., He is an "incompetent" Person.

↓

(C) A Noun Identifying a Thing Within the Person.

e.g., He has a lot of "incompetence".

Our use of language makes it so easy to make these shifts. Notice how quickly we are distracted from a focus on behavior.

Dr. Samuel pauses for a moment, sips some coffee and continues. Let's suppose you were to visit a psychology laboratory and observed a pigeon in a cage who is vigorously and persistently pecking at a disc on the wall. What conclusions might you make about the bird's behavior?"

Someone responds. "Yesterday I would have said that it is a persistent bird. But following our discussion, I can only say that I'm observing persistent behavior, and I don't know what's causing it."

Dr. Samuel replies. "That's a good answer. You focused on behavior without inferring internal causes. If you were to observe the bird for a few hours you might detect the relationship that exists between pecking behavior and its reinforcing consequences.

This relationship was mechanically pre-programed by a research psychologist so that a food reinforcer was delivered to the pigeon, on average, after every 100 pecks at the disc. Such a relationship sustains a rapid and persistent pattern of pecking. It is called a variable-ratio schedule of reinforcement (VR 100). Other schedules of reinforcement generate different patterns of behavior.

Schedules of reinforcement are very powerful variables that control our everyday behaviors. Their detection can often explain existing behaviors that appear "unexplainable".

When we don't understand behaviors, rather than admit temporary ignorance and continue to seek real causes in the environment, it is easier to infer internal causes or to create fictional explanations.

We've all encountered such "unexplainable" behaviors in "why questions". "Why don't you lose weight?" "Why don't you quit smoking?" "Why do you procrastinate?" "Why don't you get a job?" These questions beg for **an explanation of why self-defeating behaviors are repeatedly continued.**

For answers, we usually look in the wrong place. They are not found within the person. When we perceive the cause as internal, our problem is most likely to be viewed as permanent, unchangeable and untreatable. This perspective offers little optimism for change.

What sustains such self-defeating behaviors are reinforcers in the environment. To detect these reinforcers we could start with a cost-benefit analysis as already discussed. This would reveal the benefits for continuing self-defeating behaviors, as well as indicate what we would have to give up if these behaviors were to cease. In other words, a behavioral analysis will give us answers to seemingly "unexplainable" behaviors.

How would you explain the behavior of "**compulsive gamblers**"? Does the label explain anything? It explains nothing. Nevertheless, it is often offered as an explanation of behavior by reference to personality traits and internal causes. Such explanations are unproductive and have no useful value.

The reasons for gambling can be explained by finding the relationship between gambling behavior and past and present reinforcers. Reinforcers can also explain what is sustaining this repeated and persistent behavior in the present. Like the pigeon, compulsive gamblers are operating on a variable-ratio schedule of reinforcement. They gamble and lose often, but every once in awhile they win. This is enough to sustain their behavior and keep them in the game.

I don't mean to oversimplify a complex and serious problem. But be sure, it is a behavioral problem.

A personality trait is often used to explain behaviors, and the behaviors are conveniently used to justify the labeling. This sets a vicious circle in motion. Each is used to explain the other and nothing gets explained. Such misleading and unsound logic is quite characteristic of psychiatric diagnoses and labeling. It also distracts us from searching for the real causes of the behavior.

Let's consider the psychiatric diagnosis and treatment of **attention-deficit disorder**. Bruce is a ten year old child who was described by his teacher as unruly, fidgety, hyperactive, distracting and inattentive in the classroom. He was sent to a physician for help. Based mostly on the teacher's report, the physician diagnosed Bruce as having attention-deficit disorder.

The doctor prescribed methylphenidate hydrochloride, an amphetamine-like compound more commonly known as Ritalin. Such treatment implies a chemical deficiency within Bruce that is causing "undesirable" behaviors. The same negligences practiced by physicians in prescribing Prozac, also apply to the administration of Ritalin.

To refresh your memory, we talked about testing for the existence of a biochemical imbalance before prescribing a drug that is supposed to correct something that may not exist. We also talked about an inadequate collection of data to indicate whether or not the drug treatment is effective in changing behaviors in a desired direction. This would require frequent and repeated measurements of the same behaviors over time and across situations.

Needless to say, Bruce's parents were very concerned about the diagnosis and prescribed drug treatment. After all, it did come from an "expert".

When the parents spoke to the physician, he merely repeated the vicious circle answer. "I know Bruce has attention-deficit disorder because he is unable to focus attention in class." And, "The reason Bruce is unable to focus attention in class is that he has attention-deficit disorder." Hop on the merry-go-round!

I was called into the case by a friend who asked me to speak to the parents. The first thing I suggested was the "Quick and Easy Test". We discussed this earlier. **If the child really has a deficit of attention due to a biochemical imbalance, then inattention will show up in "all" situations, and not just in the classroom**. We recorded data in the home. What did we find? This same child who was inattentive in class, would often sit quietly watching television shows. Bruce also spent hours at a time glued to a computer screen on which he played games.

My assessment was that Bruce did not have a general deficit of attention. The parents were relieved and pleased to have me confirm what they already suspected. This did not, however, solve the classroom problem.

What we have here is not attention-deficit but **differential or selective attention** in specific situations.

As an environment becomes more reinforcing, attentive behavior is enhanced.

This analysis removes any mystery of attention-deficit as a disorder. It is clearly a behavioral problem, best treated by a behavioral intervention. Inattention happens to all of us in situations that lack positive reinforcement."

Someone in the group provides a supporting comment to Dr. Samuel's analysis. "I read most things very slowly. But give me a "dirty novel" or a good mystery and I become a speed reader. As you said, the more reinforcing the material, the more focused I become."

"You've got it." replies Dr. Samuel. "Can you name a few plausible explanations for inattentive classroom behavior?"

Different persons in the group respond.

"Maybe the kid isn't interested in what's being taught."

"Maybe the lessons are presented in a dull and boring way."

"Perhaps the child doesn't understand what's being taught. That may make him feel stupid and bored and not want to pay attention."

"If he's not attending to his work, I'd want to know what does have his attention. Maybe attention from classmates is more reinforcing for him than good grades."

At that point Dr. Samuel interjects. "Let's stop there. All your answers are right on track. They are pertinent to correcting Bruce's lack of attention in class.

The biggest obstacle in treatment is to get the teacher to cooperate with recommended strategies. I have no control over a teacher's behavior in a classroom. Nor do I control what is taught or how it is taught. But overall, I was lucky. Bruce's teacher was cooperative. I designed the reinforcement strategies with assistance from Bruce and the teacher. Attention improved dramatically shortly thereafter.

I want to make a few comments about **effective teaching** in the classroom. Student motivation, focus of attention, self-esteem and student performance are all by-products of positive reinforcers.

These are teacher problems. Unfortunately, the conventional thinking is to focus on them as student problems. The educational system would be better served by focusing more on teaching disabilities than on student disabilities. More focus is needed in establishing effective teaching methods.

Effectiveness can only be measured by student performance. Data is again the key. With data we can identify and discard ineffective methods and identify and keep effective methods. Without data, teaching is a game played in the dark, permitting ineffective methods to be perpetuated forever."

CHAPTER **8**

Princes, Princesses and Fairy Tale Assumptions

"Has the word **"irrational"** ever been used to refer to your behaviors, feelings or thoughts? All hands are raised.

While your conduct may be self-defeating, this does not make it irrational or illogical. If you believe something to be true, then it is real for you. You will act, think and feel as if it were real.

To others, however, your conduct may appear to be nonsensical, illogical and irrational. This is because others don't know what meaning you are attaching to the situation.

Meaning comes from two primary sources:

- First, from cues associated with previous reinforcers.
- Second, from underlying assumptions about what you, others and the world "should be like". These assumptions provide a benchmark against which to interpret what is happening. In other words, they provide meaning.

Based on these attached meanings, your actions, feelings and thoughts are very logical and rational. They make logical sense based on the assumptions that are held.

"Things" remain neutral until you attach a meaning to them.

This reminds me of a story about three umpires who were discussing how they call balls and strikes. The first umpire said, "I call 'em the way I see 'em". The second umpire said, "I call 'em the way they are". The third umpire said, "They ain't nothing until I call 'em". In other words, once called, the pitch is given meaning. Others react to that meaning as something "real" with real consequences.

Similarly, we react to meanings that we attach to things. However, sometimes you may be the only one who knows what that meaning is. Accordingly, what is logical to you, based on personal meaning, may appear illogical to others who are ignorant of that meaning.

Nevertheless, if these personally attached meanings are producing dysfunctional and self-defeating activities, they must be identified, challenged and disputed. We have already discussed meaning derived from previous reinforcers.

The focus here, will be on meaning derived from underlying assumptions that are underpinning dysfunctional behaviors, feelings and thoughts. These assumptions are usually implicit and taken for granted. In other words, they are so ingrained that we may be unaware of what they are or that we even have them.

Although unaware, we use these assumptions as comparative standards against which to judge and rate ourselves, others, and the world around us. They are perceived as real, factual and beyond challenge.

Part of the therapeutic process is to identify and make clear, obvious and explicit these sacred and implicit assumptions. Once made explicit, we can challenge and dispute their correctness and dispute the meaning attached to a violation of such assumptions.

A common underlying assumption that produces many "problems" relates **others' approval with self-worth**. The assumption is: The more approval we get from others, the more self-worth we have. If we hold this assumption and believe it to be correct, then it becomes very logical and rational to have negative self-beliefs of inadequacy and worthlessness following disapprovals, mistakes, failures and rejections.

Another extremely powerful group of underlying assumptions is what we think things "**ought to be**" like. I refer to these as "**FAIRY TALE ASSUMPTIONS**". We evaluate "what is" against an assumption of what we think "should be". Any discrepancy between the two indicates a failure to live up to expectations. How we explain this discrepancy is important. If we blame our "self", the result is self-criticism. If we blame others, the result is anger.

Reactions to violations of fairy tale assumptions are often seen in persons experiencing post-traumatic stress. Aside from the trauma of the actual experience, a part of the stress is related to an abrupt violation of what we think "should happen" and what things "should be like". Such persons often express disbelief that anything bad could or should happen to them. "Why me?" "It shouldn't have happened." "It's unfair." "People aren't nice. They're not supposed to do those things." "I don't deserve this."

Lisa ponders fairy tale assumptions. "I'm beginning to identify a lot of fairy tale expectations that have caused me much disappointment and grief. It's kinda like a "**princess mentality**".

Why do I think that everything "must" work out well? Why do I expect others and the world to cater to my wishes? I'm not a princess."

There are also fairy tale assumptions about the "**SOCIETAL ROLES**" that we play. **Roles dictate how persons "should behave", what they "should think", and how they "should feel" in specific situations**. This sets boundaries for what is expected and acceptable conduct.

When other persons do not live up to role expectations, we are disappointed and angry. As if to say, "Haven't you read the script? You're not playing "the game" the way you're "supposed to". This represents a violation of assumptions and can be upsetting.

For example, we may be upset by a mother who professes not to love her child, by a woman who can't cook, by a cowardly soldier, by a child who doesn't show respect toward a parent, by a son who doesn't cry at his mother's funeral, etc. These examples represent violations of societal role expectations for how we should behave, think and feel.

When we don't live up to role expectations, there is a tendency to blame our "self" and be self-critical.

For example, a man may feel less like a "man" if he is not financially successful and sexually potent. Another example, a woman who identifies with a caretaker role may become self-critical and experience guilt when advancing years prevent her from adequately caring for her elderly and ailing husband.

It is often a mistaken assumption that fulfilling role obligations leads to approval. It does not. This is interesting. **When role obligations are fulfilled, it is the role that often gets the credit. After all, we've merely behaved as we're "supposed to", and there's no credit in that.** Our "good" behaviors are just taken for granted. No approval. The person does, however, avoid disapproval. This makes role behavior a "safe" behavior.

On the other hand, if a role obligation is not met, the person becomes the target of blame, anger and disapproval. Disapproval for not doing what we think he/she is "supposed to do".

Whether we meet role obligations or not, we may rarely receive approval. At best, we avoid disapproval by fulfilling role obligations.

The implication of this is that many "good performances" are not positively reinforced. They are taken for granted as part of a role. This leaves many good role players with a shortage of approval and of positive reinforcers. And we know how important positive reinforcement is for good feelings and positive thoughts.

To appreciate what I have said, consider taken for granted behaviors of many women within a household: preparing meals, doing laundry, taking care of children. Such behaviors are often taken for granted and not rewarded. Likewise, many behaviors of men are also merely taken for granted as part of an expected role, and not rewarded. For example, working hard to financially support a family.

These behaviors are "expected" behaviors. However, when actual performance deviates from role expectations, it is the person who receives disapproval and blame.

This is a dangerous trap that diminishes the amount of positive reinforcement in a relationship. Don't take "good" behaviors for granted. Reinforce them. Each spouse in a relationship is an agent of positive reinforcers. Reinforcers given by one spouse will probably enhance reinforcers given by the other spouse. This results in a healthy situation of reciprocated positive reinforcement with good feelings and positive thoughts on both sides."

Fairy tale assumptions are important to an understanding and treatment of **anger**. A few words about anger are in order.

Other people and situations don't "make us" angry. We "make ourselves" angry by the meaning we attach to situations.

Two primary sources of anger are:

- First, a violation of fairy tale assumptions for how we think things "should be" and how we think others "should behave" in specific situations.

- A second source of anger is "blame" directed toward a person. If a person and behavior are seen as inseparable, we will generalize from a behavior to a rating of that person.

These two sources of anger are often combined. For example, "Kathy shouldn't speak to me in that tone." This represents a violation of what I think things "should be" like. I may then rate Kathy as an "evil person" who deserves to be punished. This may lead to feelings of anger and a subsequent verbal or physical assault.

We can challenge and dispute our fairy tale assumptions. As well, we can learn to separate person from behavior.

Two Sources of Anger:

(1) Violation of Fairy Tale Assumptions

(2) Not Separating Person and Behavior

Someone in the group asks, "**Where do fairy tale assumptions come from**?"

Dr. Samuel responds. "To answer your question, it is necessary to trace underlying assumptions through a socialization process that is influenced by a person-made social reality, societal deception and self-deception.

Underlying assumptions are first acquired early in life as part of a socialization process. They are passed on to us from many different persons in many different situations until they become generalized assumptions about what things "should be" like and how we "should" conduct ourselves. These assumptions are the building blocks of society's structure. They provide validation and legitimacy of what is "expected" and "acceptable".

Over time, these assumptions become internalized and deeply ingrained in us. You might say that the structures of society become the structures of our mind. Assumptions become taken for granted and beyond challenge. They are "givens". They just are.

There is an interesting little progression within the socialization process. Fairy tale expectations of "what ought to be" quickly translate into "what you ought to want" and finally into "what you must have".

This establishes hardened comparative standards for happiness, success and self-esteem, that usually doom us to a self-perception of failure. They are unreachable by most and unsustainable by all. "Before I can be happy or successful, I must have..."

Fairy tale assumptions establish comparative benchmarks against which we judge and rate ourselves, others and the unfolding of life. We compare "**what is**" with what we think "**ought to be**" and with "**what we must have**". Any <u>discrepancy</u> is perceived as a loss of positive reinforcement. To this loss we have learned to attach a meaning of failure, inadequacy, incompetence and low self-worth.

Expansion of Fairy Tale Expectations To "Wants" and "Needs"

Fairy tale expectations of "what ought to be" → "what you ought to want" → "what you must have" before you can be happy and successful.

Remember the story of the three umpires. "They ain't nothing until I call 'em". Well, how are you calling your game? Fairy tale assumptions will direct a meaning for you that may be self-defeating and personally harmful.

Instead of using fairy tale expectations as a benchmark for what life "should be like", may I suggest that a more practical and accurate benchmark is the **BELL-SHAPED NORMAL CURVE**.

At the end of your life, if all your experiences were plotted on a graph, we would probably get something that resembles a bell-shaped normal curve. It would reveal very few really pleasant experiences and very few really traumatic experiences. The majority would fall into a large category of hum-drum, commonplace, routine experiences. That is life.

In contrast to these expectations from a normal curve, fairy tale assumptions expect most events in life to be of the very pleasant variety, falling into the positive tail of the normal curve. This is unrealistic and will most often disappoint us.

Wishes, demands, positive expectations, and passivity won't alter the shape of the curve. Learning effective behaviors, however, can dramatically increase the frequency of positive events in our lives. Focus on improving performance without sitting in judgment of your "self". Remember, good feelings and positive thoughts are by-products of reinforcers created by good performance.

EXPECTATIONS FOR LIFE BASED ON A BELL-SHAPED NORMAL CURVE

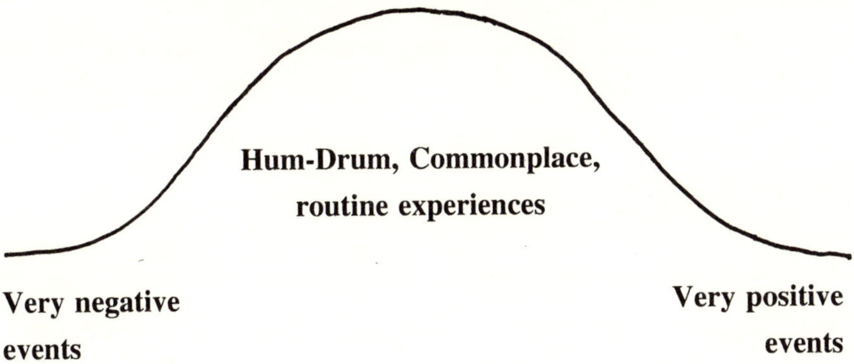

Assumptions and beliefs have been discussed as part of the socialization process. They are not part of a physical reality and their correctness cannot be readily validated in a physical sense.

Assumptions and beliefs are part of a person-made social reality that is validated by group norms. In other words, a social consensus gives validity and legitimacy to beliefs and assumptions so that they "seem" to be correct, factual and the way things "should be".

At the core of social reality is **societal deception plus self-deception**. I refer to this combination as "**REPRESSION**". This is the source of content for fairy tale assumptions. It is the source of "**Demands**".

We are deceived by society into thinking that our beliefs and assumptions about what "ought to be" are factual and proper. This is **societal deception**. For example, "a woman's place should be in the home", "women should know how to sew", "men should know about cars and sports", "marriage is the road to happiness", "your self-worth should be determined by your contribution to society", "money determines self-worth".

Over time, we internalize these societal deceptions until we believe them to be factual and legitimate. This is **self-deception**. Societal deception plus self-deception is repression.

The **concept of Repression** offers an important, valuable and enlightening framework within which we can better understand our behaviors, feelings and thoughts. Accordingly, we will elaborate more fully on this concept.

As already mentioned, repression is societal deception plus self-deception. It is perceiving and accepting a deception as the only plausible and legitimate reality. This leads to a lack of awareness of alternatives and choices. Societal deception plus a lack of awareness of this deception is what repression is about. Karl Marx called this "false consciousness". Jean-Paul Sartre called it "bad faith".

Let's compare **Oppression** with **Repression** as different ways to control masses of persons within a society.

Oppression uses coercive external forces to make persons submissive, subservient and under complete control. Such control requires much enforcement by others and accordingly is inefficient in terms of energies expended, cost and time. It may also be physically challenged and resisted.

On the other hand, there is another avenue of controlling masses of persons that is less costly and more efficient. Such control relies on deception and an internalization of that deception. This is called repression.

Persons within a society are deceived into believing that their social reality is the <u>only</u> plausible reality, and that it is inevitable and unchangeable. They forget that it is a person-made reality that has been legitimated and that other "realities" could also have been legitimated.

As people habituate to a reality over time, they begin to see it as the only plausible reality and the way things "should be", "must be" and "ought to be". Such control capitalizes on the internalization of group norms and most often goes unchallenged.

To further expand on the distinction between control by oppression and by repression - consider an illustration of a conquering army that invades and conquers new lands and people. The conquering army could enforce its laws, rules and ways of life on the conquered inhabitants by coercive measures. It could "police" the streets day and night. This would result in an enormous cost of monies, person-power and time, leaving little else for the army to do. Such control would incapacitate it from conquering other new lands.

On the other hand, the army could "sell you a bill of rules and conduct" that are in the conqueror's best interest. Over time, as you adopt and internalize these "rules", you may accept and obey them as right and necessary and not challenge them. These rules describe the way things "should be", even when they dictate differential treatment, as depicted in societal sexism and racism.

Subjugation by external control is now replaced by an internalized self-control. You no longer have to be "policed" but rather will "police" yourself because you now believe that it is the way things "should be". This is societal deception plus self-deception. It is often unchallenged and becomes the foundation of our underlying assumptions in life.

Who benefits from repression? Society benefits. The socialization process and repression are never neutral. They subtly control us and direct our behaviors into pre-determined channels deemed necessary and desirable for order to be maintained and for society to function efficiently.

What serves the best interests of society is often self-defeating for many individuals, as we've already discussed.

Let's examine **repression within societal roles**. This applies to roles with which we strongly identify. Person and the role are seen as inseparable. We perceive the role as our identity. This confuses our inner self-worth with our societal worth. The source of this confusion is repression. When we do not fulfill society's role obligations, the stage is set for self-blame, guilt, shame, perceptions of failure and inadequacy.

We do not choose to play these roles a certain way but believe that we "must" play them according to society's script. This is repression at work.

A strong identification of your "self" with roles sets up a vulnerability. For example, what becomes of your identity if the societal role ceases to exist? Consider the case of Ellen. She is a woman of forty-five years who sees herself exclusively as a wife and mother. After twenty years of strongly identifying with these roles, Ellen's husband divorced her and her child married and moved to Europe. What happens to her identity? Who is she now? Ellen's world has abruptly disintegrated. She has lost societal validation of her identity and of her self-worth. She perceives a life that is empty and without meaning.

We are more than our roles. There is a continuing "self" that transcends the roles that we play. Unfortunately the two are often confused.

It is not uncommon to hear remarks such as, "I just want to be myself", or "I want to find myself". To discover your "true self", it becomes necessary to separate a continuing "self" from societal roles, and to separate your self-worth from your societal worth. These distinctions are often blurred by societal deception and self-deception.

Becoming aware of these "perceived realities" as societal deception sets the stage for challenging their legitimacy. This attacks the very foundation of fairy tale and other underlying societal assumptions that have been held as a sacred trust."

DISCOVERING THE ROOTS OF BELIEFS AND FAIRY TALE ASSUMPTIONS

(A) Societal Deception Plus Self-Deception (Repression)

This Provides the Content of Fairy Tale Assumptions

↓

(B) Person-Made Social Reality

↓

(C) Socialization Process

↓

(D) Fairy Tale Assumptions of "What Ought To Be"

↓

(E) Discrepancy Between "What Is" and "What Ought To Be"

↓

(F) Self-Blame, Guilt, Shame, Inadequacy, Low Self-Worth

CHAPTER 9

The Human Condition is The Forgotten Assumption

"What is the human condition? As humans we have imperfections, weaknesses and fallibilities. By our essence we are "**mistake-makers**". This dictates that we will screw up many times. That is the human condition.

We have already discussed fairy tale assumptions about how things "ought to be" and how others and ourselves "ought to behave". These assumptions are based on society's script.

There is another assumption that is often forgotten or ignored. It addresses how humans "ought to behave" based on their biological essence. This is nature's script. We are forever trying to impose society's script onto nature's script. The result is a poor fit and sets the stage for perceived failure, inadequacy, self-blame and guilt.

Society demands perfection. The human condition provides imperfection. Not to remember or accept the human condition and its implications is to foolishly demand perfection from an imperfect being. When demanded of ourselves, it leads to self-blame and guilt. When demanded of others, it leads to frustration and anger.

There is a third possibility. Sometimes we demand perfection from ourselves but not from others. For example, "It's okay for others to fail, but not for me." The ancient Greeks referred to this double standard as an act of "**hubris**". It refers to a perception of self as god-like, with greater demands and expectations for self-performance than for performances of other mortals.

Society Demands Perfection.

The Human Condition Provides Imperfection.

This Results in a Poor Fit.

When Perfection is Demanded of Ourselves, it Leads to Self-Blame and Guilt. When Demanded of Others it Leads to Frustration and Anger.

I've made up an apocryphal tale regarding imperfection: Many people are not aware that we are born with a label attached to the back of our neck. It is removed at birth by the physician and reads: "Imperfection Guaranteed". Perhaps this label should not be removed. Many of us need a constant reminder, not of who we are, but of "what we are".

As humans, we most certainly will make mistakes. Many of our behaviors will be ineffective. We will not always succeed. We may not find the best solutions right away without many trials and many errors.

Unfortunately for many, failing is perceived in terms of society's script. When we do not achieve society's standards, we perceive failure. This failure is often explained as an internal inadequacy. Failure may also be perceived as a violation of an underlying assumption that we "ought to be perfect" so as to meet "perfect expectations" of society.

Failing is okay. Mistakes prove nothing about you as a person. They merely prove the validity of the human condition and reflect ineffective behaviors. It is silly to criticize and blame a person for being a "mistake-maker". That is your essence. Accept imperfections, forgive the person, and focus on changing ineffective behaviors into effective behaviors.

Failing is okay if perceived as only a behavior. As such, it is seen as temporary, changeable and specific to a situation. It needn't reflect upon the total person. Instead of passively demanding that things ought to be different, it is best to persevere and focus on improving behaviors.

Sometimes we critically judge our "self" based upon the consequences of mistakes and ineffective behaviors. Such self-blame results when we don't separate person from behavior, and don't differentiate between intentionality versus consequences of our behaviors.

If "bad" behaviors produce "bad" consequences but are unintentional, then the person may be forgiven. Unintentional "bad" behaviors can often be perceived as ineffective behaviors that occur out of ignorance, stupidity or some physical or emotional disturbance. For example, consider "bad parenting". This can have negative consequences even though it is most often unintentional. Does it make sense to blame parents under such circumstances? After all, they are also human. To demand more than that is silly.

As a general guideline, if you are the person who performed ineffectively, forgive your "self" and focus on improving your behaviors. If another person has performed ineffectively, attempt to forgive the person while focusing on changing their ineffective behaviors or just leave the situation without any attached blame or anger.

The meaning we attach to mistakes and setbacks is partially determined by whether or not we acknowledge and accept the human condition. Acceptance allows us to forgive the person and to focus on changing ineffective behaviors. Blame of the person becomes a non-issue.

Errors, mistakes and setbacks are best perceived as **feedback** about ineffective behaviors. Such feedback provides valuable information to make timely revisions until we are satisfied with our behaviors and have achieved our goals.

Without feedback, corrections could not be made. We have often heard that "practice makes perfect". This is incorrect. It is only effective behaviors that we want to strengthen through practice. However, before we know what is effective, we will often behave ineffectively. It is only trial and error, analysis and correction, that eventually leads us to effective behaviors. This process is often short-circuited by efforts to avoid failure and avoid disapproval.

Remember, failing is only a behavior. It is okay."

Forgive the Person for Being a "Mistake-Maker".

Focus on Changing Ineffective Behaviors.

CHAPTER **10**

What's So Awful?

"When we say, "**It's awful**". To what does the "it" refer?

- First, "it" represents a violation of fairy tale assumptions. "It shouldn't be that way." Well, why not? You may not "want" it to be that way, but why "shouldn't" it be that way?

- Second, the "it" refers to a discrepancy between "what is" and what we think "ought to be". "What is" represents the existing state of positive reinforcement. "What ought to be" represents an ideal state of maximum positive reinforcement. Any discrepancy between the two represents a loss of positive reinforcement. "It" refers to that loss. The perceived loss is what is awful.

In both cases we are demanding that things be other than they are. We demand that they be the way we think they "should be". These god-like demands are acts of "hubris".

"Awfulizing" Refers to Demands That Things "Ought To Be" Other Than They Are.

Obsessive Thoughts Refer to a Continuation To Demand. It is Incessant Awfulizing.

CHAPTER **11**

Obsessive Thoughts, Obsessive Thoughts and Obsessive Thoughts

"Prolonged awfulizing is obsessive thinking. It is a preoccupation with the same thoughts. These thoughts can crowd out other thoughts and interfere with daily functional activities.

Most of the time obsessive thoughts focus on a perceived loss of positive reinforcement and the meaning attached to that loss. This perception of loss is derived from a perceived discrepancy between "what is" and what we think "should be" or what we think we "must have". Preoccupations may be directed toward the past or toward the future.

There are two types of **preoccupations with the past**.

- First, there is a focus on a loss of positive reinforcement that could have potentially been gained but wasn't. This loss arises from a perceived **discrepancy between "what is" and "what might have been"**. It is usually expressed as an "if only..." statement. "If only she hadn't left me...", "If only I had asserted myself...", "If only I had stayed in the stock market...".

  In other words, "if only I had done something different in the past, my present would be so much better". There is a perceived loss of potential that might be otherwise, if only I had done things differently.

  Yes, it would be nice if we had a Time Machine to go back and correct mistakes. It would be nice if we had a magic wand. It would be nice if we were living on Fantasy Island. Demands for things gone past are merely wishful thoughts without consequence. It is a fairy tale mentality.

  Instead of wallowing in self-pity, you can seek effective behaviors that will produce positive reinforcers in the present. Don't just sit on your demands. Get involved in actions that create good feelings and positive thoughts.

- Second, another type of preoccupation with the past focuses on a loss of positive reinforcement generated by a **perceived difference between "what is" and "what used to be"**. This frequently happens when the present is characterized by an absence of positive reinforcers, good feelings and positive thoughts. In contrast, the past has all the reinforcers that the present lacks. In such circumstances it is not unusual for thoughts to gravitate toward times of greatest positive reinforcement. They were, after all, times of happy feelings and thoughts of adequacy, mastery and self-worth.

As a physical avoidance of the present is not always feasible, thought avoidance becomes an escape mechanism to better times. Such persons "live in the past", while continuing to lament the present and demand that it be other than it is.

A preoccupation with the past applies to all persons who are unhappy with their existing reinforcing environment, and has particular relevance to the elderly who are most prone to such preoccupations.

As people age into advanced years it is not unusual for levels of brain chemicals to decrease. Such depletions in elderly and depressed persons are often mistaken as the cause of the depression. They are not. Recall our earlier discussion on medication. The fact that both may be present does not mean that a chemical deficiency causes depression. It is only a <u>correlation</u> and not a cause-effect relationship.

My hunch is that most elderly persons who are depressed are suffering from an absence of positive reinforcement in their existing environments. On an individual basis this can be tested by the "Quick and Easy Method" as previously discussed. If behaviors, moods and thoughts change positively with changes in a reinforcing environment, then you'll have your answer. This will also suggest an effective and appropriate treatment intervention to reduce and eliminate the depression.

Please note that when talking about a reinforcing environment I am not referring to merely the surroundings. A joyous happy surrounding is necessary but is not sufficient to alleviate depression if it does not actively involve the depressed person. Active involvement means that positive reinforcers follow behaviors. In other words, these behaviors are effective behaviors that produce positive reinforcers. For example, speaking on a topic and having others listen with interest, telling a joke and hearing laughter, or just participating with others who display attentiveness and appreciation of your involvement.

Effective behaviors provide a sense of control over positive reinforcers. The by-products of this are feelings of happiness and thoughts of adequacy, mastery and high self-worth.

Obsessive thoughts may also be **directed toward the future**. While a preoccupation with the past focuses on a "loss of potential" positive reinforcement, a preoccupation with the future focuses on a "potential loss" of positive reinforcement. There is a **perceived loss between "what is" and "what might possibly be"**. This may be expressed by "what if..." statements and often characterizes what is meant by "worry". For example, "what if I fail...", or "what if she leaves me..."

Preoccupations with the future usually ignore the "probability" of an event occurring. Instead, they incessantly dwell on the "possibility" of its occurrence, and treat it as if it were a certainty and a "real" occurrence before it even happens. This prematurely produces bad feelings and negative thoughts before any loss actually materializes. It is the possibility of potential loss that is awfulized repeatedly.

As anything is possible, there is always a grain of truth to any "what if..." statement. We never know for sure what the future holds. That notwithstanding, we can initiate effective behaviors in the present that can somewhat enhance favorable probabilities for future events that we worry about. For example, if you're worrying about failing a test, then start preparing early. If you're worried about getting cancer, then take some preventative steps now. Eat well, don't smoke, exercise and take vitamin supplements. While no guarantees, action can enhance favorable probabilities.

Once you take action and engage in effective behaviors, your worries will diminish. You will have thoughts of control, mastery and self-reliance. Although not guaranteeing success, effective behavior does enhance its probability. In contrast, "worrying" does not alter the probability of anything. It changes nothing.

Continuing to demand that "what might possibly be" should never come to pass, can only enhance feelings of anxiety and thoughts of helplessness, hopelessness and dependency. The more you demand, the worse you feel. Incessant demanding is not only unproductive and a waste of time and energy, but most importantly it distracts us from taking effective action.

Teaching clients how to be effective is my job. It is a primary goal of therapy.

PREOCCUPATIONS

A. Preoccupation With the Past:

(a) Loss of Potential Positive Reinforcement.

Perceived Discrepancy Between "What Is" and "What Might Have Been".

"If Only..." Statements.

(b) Perceived Discrepancy Between "What Is" and "What Used To Be".

B. Preoccupation With the Future:

Potential Loss of Positive Reinforcement

Perceived Discrepancy Between "What Is" and "What Might Possibly Be".

"What If..." Statements.

What sustains obsessive thoughts, preoccupations or prolonged awfulizing? In other words, why do we continue to obsess, knowing that it keeps us feeling sad, knowing that it is self-defeating, and knowing that is doesn't produce the things we are demanding?"

Someone in the group responds. "There must be something reinforcing it."

"Exactly." replies Dr. Samuel. "That's a plausibility. Let's explore it.

The act of awfulizing may generate more attention, sympathy and comfort from others than we have been accustomed to. Although well-intentioned, these are powerful social reinforcers that can sustain self-defeating behaviors.

Overly solicitous sympathy from therapists can also reinforce a continuation of awfulizing and encourage self-pity. A client may be handed a box of tissues and be expected to begin feeling and expressing sorrows. Both client and therapist each play their role that centers around commiseration. The client expresses sorrows and the therapist expresses sympathy. While this may be temporarily comforting, it is not effective therapy. It doesn't work.

Sympathy from therapists and others may be perceived as a validation of legitimacy to continue awfulizing.

All of us enjoy receiving sympathy when we are "down". And that's okay. But it won't get us out of the stream of sorrow we are bathing in.

A perceived "right" to awfulize and wallow in self-pity can easily become a barrier that impedes a client's efforts toward change in therapy. It represents a cost of getting better and is a competing reinforcer that may be sustaining depression. This was previously discussed as part of a cost-benefit analysis used to detect a client's motivation for change.

The only comfort that really means anything will not come from others. It will come as a by-product of your own accomplishments and effective behaviors."

Lisa ponders Dr. Samuel's comments. "He seems to be talking about me. When Billy left me, I cried a lot and felt sorry for myself. As Dr. Samuel says, I demanded that things should be different and life kinder. I even expected others to comfort and take care of me. To make things better. But they only got worse. Nothing helped. Others comforted me but nobody was able to help me. Most of all, I did nothing to help myself. Nobody can come into my world and fix it. I have to do that myself. I've read a lot of self-help books. They provided temporary comfort but still left me holding my emotional baggage.

That was six months ago and I'm still demanding and self-blaming. I guess I have "fairy tale assumptions" about life and they're hurting me.

What he says makes sense. Demanding is silly. Dr. Samuel is right. The only comfort that means anything comes from my own effectiveness. All his comments about positive reinforcement are really on the mark."

CHAPTER **12**

Self-Esteem: Nature of the Problem

"When most clients are asked about their low self-esteem, answers focus on an unfavorable impression about themselves. "I don't like myself." "I'm always putting myself down." I don't have confidence in myself." I'm incompetent." "I avoid many situations and people to escape criticism. I'm afraid that I'll fail." "People treat me like a doormat. I'm afraid to stand up to them." "I'm so afraid of what others will think of me. I really want their approval."

As a follow-up question, I sometimes ask where their low self-esteem comes from. Most answers focus on internal inadequacies that are seen as unchangeable. "It's just my make-up. Must be biological." "It's part of my personality." "I've always been like this, it's just a part of me." "Some have it and some don't." "Maybe it's because of my early upbringing. But it must be irreversible by now."

It is interesting how many people attempt to account for self-esteem by looking within. They are confusing cause with effect and person with behavior, as we've already discussed.

A search for internal causes reminds me of an earlier period, hundreds of years ago, when "falling bodies" were explained by attributing a force within an object that was seeking its earthly homeland. External forces were ignored as a viable explanation for gravitational phenomena, until Newton's principles of gravitation were finally accepted by the scientific community and the public. The point is that <u>these principles had been discovered long before they were accepted</u>.

Similarly, and unfortunately, **Behavioral Principles** that quite nicely explain behaviors are often ignored today by psychiatrists and others. We are not talking theory. A behavioral analysis is exclusively and entirely empirical. It is data-based, testable and provable. It can account for the acquisition and maintenance of behaviors and offers effective strategies for behavioral change.

Although the evidence is there, many still prefer to focus on unsubstantiated inferences about internal causes. This sustains the mystery that is passed on to clients in the form of psycho-babble.

Later on I will demystify the nature of self-esteem, demonstrating that it is a by-product of reinforcers that are produced by our own effective behaviors. In other words, self-esteem is a behavioral problem.

As a focus on the "self", the issue of self-esteem is a crock. It neglects to separate person and behavior. **An impression of "self" may be based on erroneous underlying assumptions** that have been perpetuated by a socialization process, embedded within a social reality, whose content has been determined by societal and self-deception.

What are these underlying assumptions? We'll first state them, and then discuss each.

- First, many believe that a **hierarchy of human worth exists**. This implies that some people have more intrinsic self-worth than others.

- Second, many believe that **intrinsic self-worth is indicated by our societal worth**.

- Third, many believe that **self-worth is associated with approval and disapproval by others**.

In other words, we confuse perceived self-worth with varied intrinsic human worth. We also confuse intrinsic human worth with societal worth and with approval by others. Now, let's discuss each.

First, **human worth**. If we believe that individuals possess different degrees of intrinsic human worth, then we may attribute differences in performance to internal causes. This leads to a rating of others and a rating of "self" to determine whether our actual human worth is "greater than" or "less than" that of others.

A hierarchy of human worth is a fallacious assumption that cannot be proved. All of us have the same human worth that is constant and unchangeable. It does not fluctuate.

Second, **our actual human worth is confused with societal worth.** When we do not meet society's expectations, society disapproves and values us less. That is true. At times we may have less societal worth, but this does not imply that we ever have less intrinsic human self-worth.

Our societal worth is what is of value to society. For example, are we productive in the work force and paying hefty taxes? Are we married? Do we have children? Do we fulfill societal role obligations? Do our motives, values and goals correspond with what is in society's best interest?

As already discussed, societal standards are often used as benchmarks against which we compare and rate our actual performances. These standards of judgment and evaluation have been adopted and internalized as legitimate and appropriate evaluations of our self-worth.

Societal standards tell us "what ought to be". Any discrepancy between our actual performance of "what is" and societal standards of "what ought to be", indicates how well we have measured up. If these standards have not been met, we have been taught by society to see ourselves as failures, as persons of a lesser worth.

The confusion between actual human self-worth and societal worth is grounded in a person-made social reality that derives content and meaning from societal and self-deceptions.

Deception is a very powerful but subtle form of control that perpetuates institutions and roles. It greases the wheels of efficiency and provides order. We are taught to seek things that society needs and feel guilty if we do not. We have internalized "what we must have" and "what we think ought to be". Society's goals become our goals, even when they are detrimental to our well-being.

Although there isn't any objective way to measure intrinsic human self-worth, we continue to self-rate. The thought of human self-worth being constant is disturbing to many persons who "must know" if they are "better than" or "worse than" others.

If all of us accepted a constant and same self-worth, person evaluations would become non-issues and most "hang-ups" would disappear. We would then be able to focus exclusively on improving our performances.

The third underlying assumption that influences self-evaluation and self-rating is the **mistaken belief that approval and disapproval by others reflect an intrinsic human self-worth.** They do not, although they may reflect societal worth. We believe that the more approval we receive, the stronger is the validation of our intrinsic self-worth.

SOCIETY SETS UP COMPARATIVE STANDARDS AGAINST WHICH WE RATE OUR INTRINSIC SELF-WORTH.

CONFUSION BETWEEN ACTUAL SELF-WORTH AND SOCIETAL WORTH.

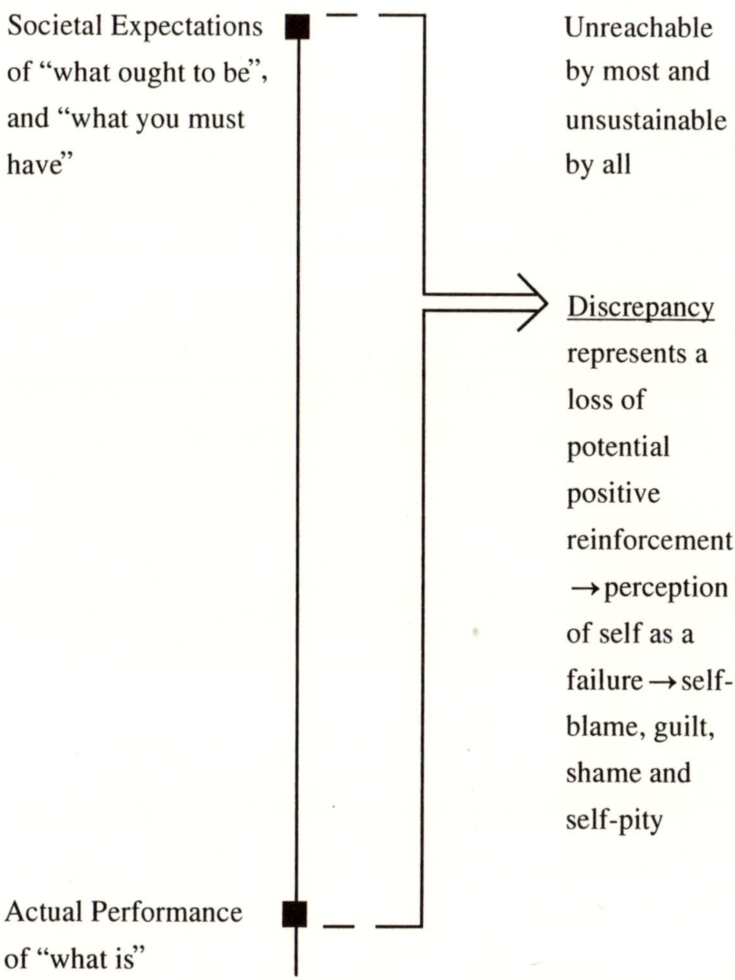

This assumption has implications of a dysfunctional nature.

- First, your conduct may be directed primarily by what you think others will approve or disapprove of. This presents an appearance of a fickle disingenuous person who checks to see which way the wind of approval is blowing before taking action. Such a preoccupation with loss of approval can produce feelings of anxiety and stress.

- Second, this assumption may lead to an avoidance of many situations in which mistakes or criticisms are anticipated. Why? Because disapproval is associated with a diminished intrinsic self-worth.

- Third, this assumption disempowers you. Instead, it empowers others over your behaviors and your perceptions of "self", and fosters a dependency upon others for a validation of your identity and intrinsic self-worth.

To appreciate the power of this assumption, imagine the following scenario: She smiled at me, my worth went up to a 7. He frowned at me, my worth dropped to a 4. I made money, up again to an 8. I lost money, down to a 3. These are fluctuations of perceived self-worth. Anything that fluctuates that much belongs on the stock exchange. It may be good for trading but not for living.

This underlying assumption that actual intrinsic self-worth is reflected by other's approval, gives importance to another implicitly held assumption: **Others "should" and "must" like me.** This is a fairy tale expectation. Where is the evidence to support the belief that others must like you, or conversely, that you must like others? Either way, would dislike "make" anyone a lesser person? Of course not.

Nevertheless, when someone doesn't like us, or even worse, rejects us, it is often disturbing. It not only represents a violation of our fairy tale expectation that they "must" like us, but more importantly, dislike and rejection are associated with a diminished intrinsic self-worth.

Dislike or rejection doesn't mean that we are lesser persons. It also doesn't mean that there must be something wrong with us. It only means that our behaviors and attributes are of little reinforcing value to a particular other with his/her preferences, biases, values, interests, etc. It doesn't imply that we will not be of reinforcing value to many other particular persons.

Part of the therapeutic process is to identify, challenge and dispute the correctness of these assumptions and the meaning attached to them.

My task is to show you how to dispute.

We previously discussed how a rating of the self is based on a faulty "generalization" from a rating of specific performances in specific situations. For example, "I failed the test and that makes me a failure." We pointed out how such a generalization neglects to separate person and behavior.

Similarly, a rating of our "total" self-worth is also based on faulty generalizations from specific behaviors. **Actual intrinsic self-worth is unmeasurable.** However, if you did attempt to measure it, what are some of the problems you may encounter?

- First, you would have to take into account "all" attributes and "all" behaviors and thoughts that not only exist but have the potential of becoming something else.

- Second, you would have to decide how attributes, behaviors and thoughts should be measured. And against what agreed-upon criteria.

- Third, what priority would you give to each measure? How are the measures to be weighted into a formula? Are brains more important than looks? Is good parenting more important than making money? And so on.

Such research is impossible. We cannot formulate a single rating of a person's intrinsic self-worth. Any attempt to do so is futile, foolish and self-defeating. Instead, focus on improving performances in specific situations."

AN EVALUATION OF INTRINSIC SELF-WORTH IS ERRONEOUSLY BASED UPON:

(a) The Underlying Assumption That a Hierarchy of Human Worth Exists.

(b) The Underlying Assumption That Intrinsic Self-Worth is the Same As Societal Worth. The Two are Confused.

(c) The Underlying Assumption That Intrinsic Self-Worth is Reflected By Approval and Disapproval of Others.

(d) A Faulty Generalization From Specific Behaviors in Specific Situations To a Single Rating of a Person's Intrinsic Self-Worth.

CHAPTER **13**

The Key to Enhancing Self-Esteem: A Viable Solution

"Intrinsic self-worth cannot be enhanced nor diminished. However, as a therapist, I can show you how to enhance your "thoughts of self-worth". After all, what is "self-esteem" if not thoughts and feelings.

High self-esteem is nothing more than feeling "up" and having thoughts of accomplishment, adequacy, competence, mastery, self-reliance and effectiveness. Ergo, thoughts of high self-worth.

On the other hand, **low self-esteem** is nothing more than feeling "down", anxious, stressful, and having thoughts of failure, inadequacy, lack of control, dependence, helplessness and hopelessness. Ergo, thoughts of low self-worth.

These feelings and thoughts are about our own effectiveness.

High self-esteem and effectiveness are highly correlated.

Think about it. When our own effective behaviors produce positive reinforcement, we have thoughts of accomplishment and high self-worth. This demystifies the nature of self-esteem.

It is not about the "self". Self-esteem is about effectiveness."

Someone asks, "Dr. Samuel, **how do we know when a behavior is effective**?"

"You'll know by the consequences of that behavior. If the outcome or experience is positively reinforcing, it will be accompanied by good feelings, positive thoughts, and you'll want to see more of that experience.

On the other hand, if the experience is negative, you'll know that your behavior was ineffective. The experience will be accompanied by bad feelings and negative thoughts. It will be an experience you won't want repeated. If it's presently occurring, you'll want it terminated. And in the future you'll avoid similar experiences.

BEHAVIOR	**→**	**CONSEQUENCES**
Effective Behavior	**→**	**feeling "up" and thoughts of mastery and accomplishment. Ergo, high self-worth.**
Ineffective Behavior	**→**	**feeling "down", anxious and thoughts of inadequacy, dependency, lack of control, helplessness. Ergo, low self-worth.**

Before we can enhance self-esteem, we must first demystify its nature and remove the psycho-babble surrounding it. This has already been done.

Second, we must define self-esteem in measurable units so that we will know exactly "what" we are enhancing, and whether or not intervention strategies have enhanced it.

On a ten-point scale, clients rate good feelings, positive thoughts and rate the effectiveness of their performance in specific situations. **Data. Data. Data.** This not only indicates any changes in thoughts of self-worth but also allows us to identify specific situations, tasks and persons that are associated with thoughts of high and low self-worth.

Effectiveness is of primary importance in generating thoughts of high self-worth. It is most important to remember that effectiveness is <u>specific to situations</u> and is not a generalized personality trait. In other words, you may be effective in some situations and not in others.

That notwithstanding, the more situations in which you are effective, the more generalized and stable are your thoughts of self-worth.

In therapy, effectiveness is taught within many different situations at home, at work and socially.

In addition to effectiveness, it is also important, when possible, to re-arrange, select or choose an environment that readily reinforces your behaviors. This applies to a work environment, leisure activities or to the selection of friends and spouses. For example, if you want to think of yourself as intelligent, then don't surround yourself with persons who always put you down. If you enjoy telling jokes, don't surround yourself with persons who don't appreciate your humor. Select a reinforcing environment that will have a positive impact on your thoughts of self-worth.

While clients may want to be effective, there may be barriers that impede efforts toward this goal. These must be identified, disputed and removed. A cost-benefit analysis is helpful.

There may be a fear of failing and a fear of embarrassment. There may be a fear of behaving in a new way that is "uncharacteristic of me". "What will people think?" Such fears must be removed before clients can be expected to attempt new effective behaviors.

Merely giving clients advice and telling them to do what you think is best for them is not sufficient. It is the therapists task to enhance a client's motivation to want change and to attempt new effective behaviors."

IDENTIFYING BARRIERS THAT MAY IMPEDE ATTEMPTS AT NEW EFFECTIVE BEHAVIORS

<u>Not</u> attempting New Effective Behaviors		**Attempting New Effective Behaviors**	
<u>Costs</u>	**<u>Benefits</u>**	**<u>Costs</u>**	**<u>Benefits</u>**

Someone asks Dr. Samuel a question. "Would we still have thoughts of high self-worth if we received a lot of positive reinforcers that were unearned? That is, without effective behaviors."

Dr. Samuel responds. "Thoughts of high self-worth are not correlated with positive reinforcement, per se. They are correlated with effective behaviors that produce positive reinforcers. The positive reinforcers must be perceived to be dependent upon <u>our own</u> behaviors. Only then, do we have thoughts of mastery and accomplishment, and accordingly, thoughts of high self-worth.

Let's consider some examples. A beautiful young woman, or a handsome young man may receive much attention and many compliments. While the recipients of much positive reinforcement, they may still have low self-esteem and may even suffer with depression.

The positive reinforcers are related more to an attractive appearance than to an effective performance. In other words, these gorgeous persons have little control over the positive reinforcers in their lives. Accordingly, they may feel "down" and have thoughts of inadequacy, dependency and helplessness. There are no thoughts of effectiveness and accomplishment.

Thoughts of High Self-Worth Are Correlated With Effective Behaviors That Produce Positive Reinforcement In the Present.

Thoughts of low self-worth may be further accentuated with advancing age. As their beauty disappears, so do the reinforcers that were dependent upon appearance. This vulnerability of eventual loss is avoided when positive reinforcers are based upon current effectiveness.

Let's consider another example. There are many persons who have been productive and effective in the past but no longer are. They may continue to receive much positive reinforcement based on past accomplishments, but not for current performances. Such persons may experience low self-esteem and depression. This is sometimes seen with retirees, former athletes and former movie stars. It can, however, happen to anyone.

What about persons who have inherited wealth that they did not earn? This is a similar story. The money alone does not guarantee high self-esteem. Thoughts of high self-worth are based upon our own effectiveness and not upon the reinforcers we possess.

If you had thoughts of incompetence but were to win a million dollar lottery, would that change your thoughts of self-worth? Probably not. While you may feel euphoric, you would now think of yourself as a "rich incompetent". While wealth, whether earned or unearned, represents societal worth, only our own current effectiveness is correlated with thoughts of accomplishment and high self-worth.

Wealth Alone, Represents Societal Worth. Only Our Own Effectiveness In The Present is Correlated With Thoughts of Accomplishment and High Self-Worth.

We are often dismayed when we hear that beautiful persons, formerly successful persons, or wealthy persons are suffering with low self-esteem and depression. A plausible reason is that they lack control over positive reinforcers in their present environments. In other words, they lack current effectiveness.

It is important to do things for yourself, be self-reliant and create positive reinforcers through your own effectiveness. When others do things for you, you are being robbed of opportunities to have good feelings and positive thoughts about your own effectiveness. Such seemingly benign nurturing by others often fosters thoughts of incompetence, dependency, helplessness, and eventually low self-worth.

I'm going to tell you a personal story. For years my mother had her taxes prepared by an accountant. Although her taxes were straight-forward and simple, she perceived the task as overwhelming and felt incompetent to handle it. One year I persuaded her to fill out the forms.

To make it easier, we decided to use the previous year's form as a role model. Where the accountant had a number, we put a new number, and so on. The task was completed and my mother had a great sense of mastery and accomplishment. This was in stark contrast to preceding years where mother was left with thoughts of dependency and helplessness."

Another question from someone in the group. "Can successful people ever have thoughts of low self-worth? You've discussed people who appear successful to others, yet not to themselves. You mentioned those with beauty, past accomplishments and wealth. But what about people, for example, who are very effective and successful at their job? Can they have low self-esteem?"

Dr. Samuel responds. "The answer is 'yes'. Let's examine three plausible conditions in which that might occur.

First, remember that effectiveness is specific to situations. Persons may perceive themselves as effective and successful in some areas of their lives, but not in others. For example, a successful business woman may say to herself, "Although I'm very rich, and am successful and productive at the office, I am nothing unless I'm loved."

What about a father who earns very little money, yet spends much quality time with his children? Although he may see himself as an effective and good parent, nevertheless, he may also perceive himself as a failure for not earning more money. He has obviously accepted society's criterion for success.

In therapy, the assumptions underlying these self-critical beliefs are identified and disputed. As well, clients select goals for effective behaviors in specific situations and areas of their lives in which they were previously ineffective. The attainment of such goals is targeted as part of the therapeutic process.

Second, successful persons may have low self-esteem based on the criteria they choose for self-evaluation. You will always be able to compare your "self" or your performance with someone who is richer, smarter, more productive, etc. This guarantees a self-perception of failure and is self-defeating.

Third, successful persons may attribute their accomplishments to luck or accident, and not to their own effective behaviors. For example, "I'm still the same incompetent person. It's just that I had some lucky breaks," or "Others who praise me are fooled. They don't know me well enough. If they did, they would see that I'm really quite incompetent. I can't even change a light bulb at home."

Perhaps in this example, as well as previous ones, there is an underlying assumption that competence and effectiveness "should generalize" across all situations. This is a belief in a personality trait. It focuses on "something within the person" that should transcend all situations and environmental influences. It does not.

Effective behaviors are specific to situations and do not generalize well across dissimilar situations. There is a confusion between person and behavior. In therapy, this assumption is made explicit, then challenged and disputed.

We have identified **three solutions to the problem of low self-esteem**:

- First, challenge the perceived inseparableness of person and behavior. Once separated, self-evaluations and self-ratings are greatly reduced. Self-blame, guilt, shame, embarrassment become non-issues.

  The primary focus is to improve performance without a fear that failing behaviors reflect a diminished self-worth.

- Second, identify and dispute assumptions that underlie unfavorable impressions of self-worth.

- Third, create good feelings and positive thoughts through effective behaviors that produce positive reinforcement. Remember, effectiveness in the present is correlated with thoughts of high self-worth."

THREE SOLUTIONS TO THE PROBLEM OF SELF-ESTEEM

1. **Separate Person and Behavior.**

   This Reduces Self-Evaluations and Self-Ratings.

   Focus Exclusively on Improving Performances.

2. **Dispute Assumptions That Underlie Unfavorable Impressions of Self-Worth.**

3. **Create Effective Behaviors That Produce Positive Reinforcers.**

   Effectiveness in the Present is Correlated With Thoughts of High Self-Worth.

CHAPTER **14**

What Is Happiness?

"We've all been asked at one time or another, "Are you happy?" This can be a puzzling question to many.

What is happiness? It's really not that difficult to define. Think about it. Is happiness anything more than good feelings and positive thoughts? These are effects or by-products of positive reinforcers.

Likewise, unhappiness can be defined as bad feelings and negative thoughts. These are effects of a loss or absence of positive reinforcers.

Is Happiness Anything More Than Good Feelings and Positive Thoughts?

These are By-Products of Positive Reinforcers.

This knowledge can empower you. It enables you to "make yourself" happy, or at least minimize unhappiness, by seeking out reinforcing environments and by creating positive reinforcers through your own effectiveness.

We've already discussed effectiveness as being specific to situations. The same applies to happiness. It is not only situation-specific but is also temporary. Happiness does not come from within a person but is produced by reinforcers in the environment. It is a by-product of reinforcers that we experience.

Likewise, unhappiness does not come from within. It may be best treated not as an internal problem, not as a personality problem, but as a behavioral problem.

In therapy, all clients fill out a weekly form on happiness in specific situations as well as an over-all measure of "General Happiness". Each is rated on a ten-point scale. These data allow us to identify areas of unhappiness, to measure the effectiveness of intervention strategies toward happiness, and to indicate progress over time. **Data. Data. Data.**

Sometimes, as an exercise between sessions, I'll ask clients to record "**HAPPIES**" on a golf counter. Each "HAPPIE" is a good feeling or positive thought. It represents a positive reinforcer.

There are three parts to this **exercise**:

- First, clients are asked to become more aware and notice positive reinforcers in their environment. These may come from an appreciation of our surroundings and from other persons. Quite often we lose an awareness of positive reinforcers that surround us. Attending and becoming aware of them will make explicit what was previously implicit, unnoticed and taken for granted.

- In the second part of the exercise, clients are asked to record positive reinforcers that have been created by their own effective behaviors.

- In the third part, clients are asked to look for patterns of recurring positive reinforcers in different situations, activities, and with different persons. This focuses attention and awareness on the sources of good feelings and positive thoughts, which clients may have previously been unaware of.

Recordings of positive reinforcers are done both on a golf-counter and in a journal. The golf-counter provides a readily accessible frequency measure that serves as valuable data. Journal entries may be more profitably used for detailed descriptions and analyses.

The therapeutic value of this exercise is to <u>enhance the density of positive reinforcers</u> in the client's life. This is done by increasing awareness of existing reinforcers and by creating new reinforcers through effective behaviors.

Remember, you can create your own happiness. You don't have to rely on others to "make you" happy. In many relationships, there is often a tendency to demand that the other "make us happy". If you give others the power to make you happy, they will also have the power to make you unhappy.

While positive reinforcers are crucial to happiness, it is even better if they come from many different sources. This can lessen the impact of a loss from any one source, thereby creating less of a void in your life.

From this perspective, let's examine thoughts of **suicide**. Such thoughts may occur when:

(a) there is a perceived absence of positive reinforcers from all sources and in all segments of one's life, and

(b) there is a perceived helplessness to alter these conditions of loss, as well as a perceived hopelessness that change is possible. It is a perception of living in a world that no longer exists.

Suicide attempts may be deterred by offering some plausibility for change. Even better if some positive reinforcement can be restored in just a few segments of an otherwise perceived empty existence. This may be sufficient to establish optimism for additional positive reinforcers and further change. Such efforts may temporarily save a life and provide borrowed time to implement effective therapeutic interventions."

CHAPTER **15**

Repeated Measurements, Data, Goals and Treatment Interventions

---

"Throughout our talk, I have repeatedly emphasized the importance of **DATA**. I'm going to elaborate on this and show you how data are collected and made meaningful. The method of collection we'll discuss is what is used by the scientific community.

First, prior to any treatment interventions, measurement scores are obtained from a few tests, such as the Beck Depression Inventory (BDI) and a Happiness Rating Scale. This takes about five minutes and is completed at the beginning of each session. <u>Repeated measures</u> are obtained from these tests throughout therapy. Measurements are also recorded from other tests that are only completed in the first session and at the end of treatment.

Repeated measures on the same tests serve as a **base-line** against which to evaluate client progress and the effectiveness of treatment strategies. They also alert the therapist to interventions that are ineffective and require timely revisions.

After "problems" have been identified and defined in behavioral units, treatment strategies are planned. Before these strategies are implemented, however, certain base-line measures of "problem behaviors" are taken. For example, a client may have expressed feelings and thoughts of anxiety, inadequacy, embarrassment, and incompetence in a previous situation. For base-line purposes, the client is asked to rate this past experience in that specific situation on three dimensions.

He/she rates on a ten-point scale:

(a) how effective his/her performance was,

(b) good feelings,

(c) positive thoughts.

Consider a case of non-assertiveness. Henry rated the effectiveness of his previous performance in the specific situation we were targeting as 3/10, good feelings as 2/10, and positive thoughts as

2/10. Henry's ineffective performance led to negative reinforcers and their by-products, namely, bad feelings and negative thoughts.

The **intervention strategy** was to teach Henry how to be assertive in this situation and motivate him into action.

Following the intervention strategy, Henry was again asked to rate the effectiveness of his <u>new</u> performance, as well as his feelings and thoughts. These measurements are called **post-treatment measures**.

The results were as follows:

(a) rating of effective performance 8/10,

(b) good feelings 10/10,

(c) positive thoughts 10/10.

These data indicate three things:

- First, they show an improvement over initial base-line measures.

- Second, they demonstrate effectiveness of the treatment intervention. If data had indicated very little positive change, then timely revisions in treatment would have been made.

- And third, the results indicate a strong relationship between effective performance and good feelings, positive thoughts.

We were on the right track and knew it. This was also corroborated by Henry's Depression Score improving dramatically.

Frequent and repeated measurements are essential to effective therapy. This also applies when the treatment is a drug.

Unfortunately, most psychiatrists, physicians and therapists do not systematically record data. They operate in the dark and their results most often indicate as much, both in terms of effectiveness and extended duration of therapy.

Short-term and long-term goals are also a part of effective therapy. They are established in collaboration with clients and are directed toward behaviors in different situations at work, at home and socially.

Goals must be realistic, attainable and stated in measurable units. This allows us to record repeated measures of progress toward desired goals, and to indicate what percentage of goal attainment has been achieved at any time throughout therapy.

SCIENTIFIC METHODOLOGY

A. Initial Base-Line Measures (Pre-Treatment)

B. Treatment Intervention

C. Post-Treatment Measures

There are two primary treatment interventions that we'll discuss - a Behavioral Intervention and a Disputation Intervention.

The **BEHAVIORAL INTERVENTION** targets performance of new effective behaviors in specific situations where ineffective behaviors were previously performed.

This often requires the teaching and repeated practice of new behavioral and social skills before actual performance is attempted. As well, any barriers that might impede efforts toward success are identified and eliminated.

The importance of a good effort is emphasized over a concern about actual accomplishment. In my clinical practice, I have found that a client's good initial effort in the real world, even without complete success, leads to good feelings and positive thoughts. Good efforts and corrections of those efforts eventually produce complete success. Setbacks are nothing more than behavioral problems. They are temporary and changeable.

Behavioral interventions enhance effectiveness and positive reinforcers in a client's life. As by-products, the client will experience good feelings of "upness" and positive thoughts of control, mastery, accomplishment and high self-worth.

The second primary intervention strategy is **DISPUTATION**. Clients are taught to challenge and dispute (a) dysfunctional, self-defeating beliefs, and (b) fairy tale and other underlying assumptions that give "meaning" to these beliefs.

It is also important to get clients to examine the source of underlying assumptions. This has been discussed earlier.

Underlying assumptions arise from an unquestioning acceptance of a social reality about how things "ought to be". The core of this social reality is societal deception and self-deception. These deceptions provide "content and meaning" to underlying assumptions that are taken for granted.

Clients are taught to question and challenge the legitimacy of a social reality which was previously accepted as "factual" and sacrosanct. As they do so, the facades of social institutions begin to disintegrate. Deceptions are seen as deceptions and are no longer perceived as a sacred reality of the way things "ought to be".

There are **two components of a Disputation**:

- The first focuses on the correctness of what we believe.
- The second focuses on the meaning attached to what we believe.

How correct are our beliefs and underlying assumptions? Their correctness and appropriateness are often implicitly taken for granted. However, just because you believe something, does not make it factual.

We usually seek out confirmation and support for our beliefs and ignore evidence that invalidates and disproves them. In other words, we don't allow our taken-for-granted opinions, even negative ones, to be clouded by evidence that might prove our beliefs false or at least cast doubt on their validity.

Clients are taught to empirically test any self-defeating beliefs.

TREAT YOUR BELIEFS NOT AS "FACTS" BUT AS HYPOTHESES TO BE TESTED EMPIRICALLY BY ALL THE EVIDENCE.

WHAT DO THE DATA SAY? SPEAK ONLY FROM THE DATA.

Have you taken into account evidence that disproves and invalidates your "negative beliefs"? Have you considered alternative and plausible interpretations of what you believe to be factual?

When critically examining your "self" as a failure, have you ignored many successful performances, only to focus on a few failing performances? In other words, have you focused on a small "frequency" of "bad" behaviors and ignored the "proportion" of "bad" to "good" behaviors? Perhaps you didn't even count "good" behaviors, which may have been taken for granted and ignored.

Have you made sweeping and faulty generalizations about your "self" based on only a few behaviors? Did you make the mistake of perceiving person and behavior as inseparable?

When examining the validity of a belief, pretend you are Spock from Star Trek. In other words, remove your biases and emotional baggage in any analysis and speak only from evidence. Speak only from the data. Let the data speak. This may provide evidence that casts doubt on a self-defeating belief and questions its validity. Seek it out. Seek out evidence that disproves and invalidates "negative" beliefs.

Clients are also taught to challenge the correctness and validity of fairy tale and other underlying assumptions. Where is the evidence that something "ought to be"? While these assumptions are taken for granted, where is the evidence to support them?

The second component of a Disputation is to challenge the meaning attached to "negative" beliefs. To do so, it is necessary to make explicit the sources of this meaning.

Interpretation of beliefs and their meaning come from underlying assumptions that have been internalized within a socialization process that is never neutral. The meaning and content of assumptions are derived from our social reality that is shaped by societal deception and self-deception.

By revealing the "sources" of meaning, clients learn how the meanings that shape their reactions have been acquired, how they are sustained, and what is the societal agenda for "pushing" certain beliefs, values, etc.

The first component of a Disputation targets the correctness and validity of beliefs and underlying assumptions. The second component targets their legitimacy by challenging societal meanings attached to them.

Most often, evidence can be found that invalidates and disproves the correctness of "negative" beliefs. There are times, however, when "negative" beliefs are correct. For example, "My wife no longer loves me."

In such situations it becomes important to challenge and dispute the "**meaning of awfulness**" that has been attached to these beliefs. While such an event is unfortunate and perhaps inconvenient, where is the evidence that it is awful?

Perhaps your wife doesn't love you. Does that make you unlovable to others? Of course not. Does it mean that you will not find another "one and only"? Of course not. You may meet many "true loves". Does your loss doom you to unhappiness forever? Of course not. There are other sources of positive reinforcement that exist or can be created by your own effective behaviors.

At this point, if I've hit a nerve, you may be saying to yourself, "Ya, but you don't understand. I really need her/him. What you say may work with others, but not with me." Nonsense. Don't treat your "problem" as unsolvable and don't continue to self-pity and awfulize about it. Take action and create positive reinforcers in your life. Focus on solutions to problems and not merely on the problems.

Also, look around, take inventory, and treasure the reinforcers that already exist. I'm not saying it's easy, but it is workable.

We have discussed Behavioral interventions that target new effective behaviors, and Disputation interventions that target meaning and legitimacy.

Quite often in therapy, verbal disputations are necessary before clients can be expected to attempt new effective behaviors.

Consider "assertiveness", for example. Before clients can be expected to stand up for their "rights", they must first believe that they have rights. These persons usually have thoughts of low self-worth. These thoughts of worthlessness must first be challenged and disputed before attempting new effectiveness in specific situations."

DISPUTATIONS

(A) Challenge and Prove False the Correctness of Beliefs and Their Underlying Assumptions.

(B) Challenge the Meaning and Interpretation Attached to Beliefs.

(C) Challenge the Legitimacy of Underlying Assumptions and Their Sources - Social Reality, Societal Deception and Self-Deception.

(D) When "Negative" Beliefs are Correct, Challenge and Prove False Any "Meaning of Awfulness" Attached to Those Beliefs.

CHAPTER **16**

Lisa's Comments and Therapy

"Dr. Samuel wrapped up his presentation and thanked everyone for attending. We all gave him a big round of applause, to which he smiled and said, "What gorgeous noise."

I guess that was his reinforcer. We all need plenty of those. One of the many things I've learned tonight is the importance of positive reinforcement.

I think everyone took one of his cards before leaving. Some even took a few. Probably for friends. As for myself, I'm definitely going to call Dr. Samuel in the morning and make an appointment. I like his approach, personal style and enthusiasm. It's refreshing. What he says makes so much sense.

I'm beginning to see my problems in a different light. They're manageable and treatable. I feel very optimistic about getting rid of this depression that has been ruining my life."

A week later Lisa started therapy.

Lisa's depression indicated a loss of control over positive reinforcers in many areas of her life. There was a general unhappiness with her present environments and a sense of helplessness to change them. Her problems included difficulties with a domineering mother, self-blame, guilt, unassertiveness and thoughts of inadequacy and low self-worth.

After attending the Thursday night talk, Lisa no longer perceived her depression as an unchangeable part of her. Problems were now viewed as temporary and treatable. She was motivated to work for change and optimistic about recovery.

My time spent with Lisa was simply to show her how to rethink her problems and how to apply the concepts, principles and intervention techniques to the details of her life situations.

Progress was swift and was documented with, and guided by data. Therapy took only a few sessions before Lisa's Depression Inventory Score was healthy-normal and desired personal goals were achieved.

Lisa learned how to challenge the correctness and meaning of her fairy tale assumptions. She also learned how to behave effectively in specific situations. This expanded the number of positive reinforcers in her life. It also enhanced good feelings and thoughts of self-worth about her accomplishments. Lisa's depression had been eliminated.

Following the termination of therapy, I received several phone calls from Lisa enthusiastically telling me how she was solving problems as they occurred.

About a year later, as part of a formal follow-up, I contacted Lisa to see how she was doing. This provided valuable data about Lisa's sustained progress over time. It also indicated long-term effectiveness of the intervention strategies used in therapy.

Improvements made during therapy were not only maintained, but Lisa was making additional gains in her life using the concepts and techniques she had been taught in therapy.

Our conversation was upbeat and positive. We were both very pleased with the outcome.

Effectiveness of treatment and its lasting benefits have nothing to do with the duration of therapy. Progress can only be achieved and sustained by disputing self-defeating beliefs and their underlying assumptions; by changing behaviors so that they are more effective; and by changing environments so that they are more positively reinforcing. This can be accomplished within a very short period of time, and will endure as long as the "new behaviors" lead to positive reinforcement. **Remember, it is the consequences of our actions that control behavior, feelings and thoughts.**

As something ends, something else begins. "Good things" will begin that much sooner with your efforts to create positive reinforcers. The power is yours "to make things happen".

Become effective, and help others to become effective.

TO MY READERS

I'd be delighted to hear from you regarding personal comments, general comments, suggestions, what was particularly helpful, etc.

You may contact me by writing to:

Dr. Michael John Frank
c/o BridgeRock Press,
197 Strathearn Road,
Toronto, Ontario, Canada.
M6C 1S3

Recorded messages may be left by calling
(416) 375-1943.

Michael John Frank earned an M.A. from Columbia University and a Ph.D. from the University of Minnesota. Both degrees are in psychology. Today Dr. Frank is a cognitive behavioral therapist and consultant in private practice in Toronto, and is available for workshops, presentations, consultations and private therapy sessions.

Personal Notes

Personal Notes